Grants for History 2014

A Guide to Funding

John R Davis
with Zoe Holman and
Maureen McTaggart

Institute of Historical Research
School of Advanced Study
University of London

2013

INSTITUTE
OF HISTORICAL
RESEARCH

University of London
School of Advanced Study

Published by
Institute of Historical Research
School of Advanced Study
University of London
Senate House, London WC1E 7HU

© University of London 2013

ISBN 978 1 905165 95 7
ISSN 1359-1126

Contents

Introduction
1   About this *Guide*   v
2   How to use the *Guide*   vii
3   How to apply for funding   viii
4   Useful addresses and further links   x
5   Errors, experiences and additions   xiii

Funding Sources
1   Conference grants   1
2   Fieldwork and heritage   5
3   Guest fellowships and relocation   9
4   Library research grants   35
5   Miscellaneous awards   51
6   Postdoctoral awards   57
7   Postgraduate awards   65
8   Prizes   89
9   Publications grants   109
10   Research grants   113
11   Travel grants   133

Index
References are to award numbers, not pages
1   Index of awards   139
2   Index of awarding bodies   149
3   Geographical index   155
4   Subject index   157

Introduction

1   About this *Guide*

The fourteenth *Guide* to funding for history

From the start, the aim of the *Guides* series has been to provide historians based in Britain with authoritative and up-to-date information about financial resources for research, and thereby support them in an environment of increasingly independent (i.e., non-state) and competitive funding. Since they began in 1997, the *Guides* have, however, widened their scope to include a broad range of related historical disciplines (e.g., archival, conservationist, heritage). The *Guides* are one component of the IHR's publications portfolio, which provides an overview of historical research culture, both in Britain and internationally.

As far as possible, in addition to on-going, near-permanent sources of money, the present volume has incorporated the latest information about funding likely to become available in 2014–15. Efforts have been made to contact funding bodies to find out about planned schemes, but inevitably a good deal of guesswork has been involved. A plea, therefore, is made to anyone intending funding in the near future to consider these volumes as a means of advertisement.

The task of drawing together a volume on funding for historical research successively over a period of several years enables general conclusions to be drawn on the national picture regarding historical research funding. In the second volume of this series, the impact of the web was noted. This has long since established itself as the primary source of information on funding, as well as of the associated tasks of downloading forms, submitting enquiries, and putting in bids. The number of dedicated websites for finding funding has increased – as demonstrated by the substantial list below. Generally, the whole process of funding has moved decisively towards web-based activities.

More recently, it was noted that funding was becoming more targeted. The number of awards concerned with particular projects seemed to be on the increase; possibly relating to a new emphasis among the research councils on specific areas of research; possibly also correlating to the development of research clusters at universities. Such clustering and national and international collaboration, and dissemination techniques often involving the web, all appear to be current priorities of research funders.

A final point: despite the universality of the web, and the increasing provision by universities of websites listing useful sources, it is remarkable just how opaque university websites are themselves when it comes to internal funding sources. One wonders why institutions make it so difficult for their own researchers to find out what resources are available. Top-class research demands competition and high-quality applications. With higher education becoming ever more dependent on non-government funding sources, and the international competition for research provision growing, it is important to maintain a high degree of transparency regarding funding possibilities. This thought also lies behind these volumes.

Who is the *Guide* for?

The main condition upon which funding sources have been included in the *Guide* is that they specifically support research in history, and affiliated research activities, and that they are open to historians based in Britain, as well as to those intending to base their research here. Those seeking funding sources for undergraduate study, for postgraduate taught courses, for teaching of history at school, college or university, or in order to develop curricula and so on, will unfortunately have to look at other relevant directories. However, this *Guide* will be useful to:

• Those hoping to do postgraduate research related to history
• Those who are intending to supervise or encourage postgraduate research
• Postgraduates doing research and looking for financial support
• Supervisors of postgraduate research
• Academic staff of all grades looking for monies for individual research
• Academic staff of all grades looking for support for institutional/joint research
• Independent (i.e., non-affiliated) historians seeking financial support
• Professors/Research co-ordinators
• Conference convenors
• Those intending to hold a temporary research institute
• Directors of research institutes
• Archivists, curators and librarians

The purposes for which they may be seeking financial support include:

• Tuition, maintenance and travel support for postgraduate research courses
• Dissertation or research course completion
• Travel involved in research
• Maintenance involved in research
• Research publication costs
• Archival visits
• Library visits
• Writing up
• Conference convening
• Conference attendance
• Field work
• Attendance at an accredited research centre or institute
• Offsetting expenses already incurred
• Professional training/development in primary source management

2 How to use the *Guide*

Two points

a) One of the main purposes of the *Guides* is to help researchers find appropriate funding as quickly and efficiently as possible. Those sources are indicated which are definitely open to historians because they have signalled themselves to be so. However, not all funds that are 'out there' and which are available to historians are included here. For one thing, there are many funds open to a wide range of disciplines to which historians may also apply. Also, history, by dint of its universally inclusive nature, shades into numerous other disciplines. Where historians have time, therefore, they should still try to look for more generally applicable funds which may cover their area of interest.

Remember:

Historical research, for example, usually can be thought of as 'the history of A' or 'the history of B'. Researchers would do well, therefore, to look at the fields of A and B too. Historians of medicine or art, for example, may more fruitfully search directories of medical or artistic funding sources than those of history.

Similarly, many history researchers work on subjects related to a particular geographic area. Here, too, research funds may be available for work connected to the geographic area, rather than to history. Check in other directories under the name of the area you are researching. Also get in touch with relevant embassies/consulates – many countries encourage foreign interest through their representatives abroad.

If you are thinking of studying for a postgraduate research degree at a particular institution of higher education, or if you are thinking of going there as a visiting scholar, get in touch with that institution's admissions department and enquire about internal bursaries/scholarships/funds etc. Many universities, institutes and so on run their own funding schemes and often have bilateral arrangements with charities and trusts.

Do not forget the internal route: if you are employed or affiliated to an institution of higher education there may be funds available to you for research, even if increasingly viewed as a last resort. There are also often staff development funds which might be used to support research. Certain historical and other societies also occasionally have funds which are only open to their members.

The first rule, then, is to think laterally.

b) Use this *Guide* simply as a starting point, and not just because there are far more funding sources out there than can be listed here. The original intention of these *Guides* was to set out enough information for historians to be able to go on and take the next step themselves. With the introduction of annual volumes and the increasing number of sources cited, citations have been more strictly limited to providing brief overviews and contact details of funding sources. Once an award or fund of interest has been found, a letter, a telephone call, fax or email message, or more often the relevant website will provide further information and application forms. The information contained in this *Guide* has been whittled down to what historians need to know to start off with. Thereafter, the ball is in their court.

Getting around the *Guide*

First, look at the Subject Index. Here are listed some of the main areas of historical interest. Look and see if yours is included.

If it is: note down the references given. Entries are numbered consecutively throughout the *Guide*, and references are to these numbers, not to pages.

If it is not: do not panic. Scout first through the funding sources listed under related headings, and under the headings 'History, general' and 'Unrestricted'. Then simply go through the *Guide* page by page – you may come up with something relevant, or even something you had not thought of before!

Note when using the *Guide* that in order to avoid problems when it comes to making the application, American spelling has been retained as in the original. This might make a difference when searching for a particular funding source.

3 How to apply for funding

There are many works available for those who wish to read up first on the process of grant application as well as many websites (see below). Nevertheless, the increasing frequency of workshops at higher education institutions and elsewhere on the issue of applying for funding suggests a) that ever more pressure is being brought to bear on academics to find independent funding, and b) that academics themselves still feel rather unsure about the process of application and in need of some guidelines.

Because of this (and with apologies to those who are already experienced in the realm of application procedures) some basic rules of thumb should be given regarding the procedures to be followed, gleaned from introductions to existing directories, and the experiences of academics and those on the awarding committees of funding bodies as expressed at the workshops above-mentioned:

a) Read the guidelines produced by the funding body

This is important. No matter what information is given here, funding bodies can best tell you themselves the requirements for application. Deadlines, how many forms need to be completed, numbers and nature of referees, tenability, accessibility and provision of funds change from fund to fund as well as from time to time. Make sure that you have chosen the right funding body for your area of research. If in doubt about this, do not hesitate to contact the body and ask.

b) Put as little burden on the funding body as possible

Complete the application form in the way required. Do not deviate from instructions (behind them may lie complicated processing procedures). Make sure referees are informed clearly of deadlines and will get their submissions in on time. Write neatly and, if possible or required, type your application. Include a stamped and addressed envelope in an initial approach to the funding body – many charities and smaller funding bodies have limited resources and cannot afford to respond if you do not.

c) Avoid poor communication

Be clear, concise and direct in all aspects of your application. Be absolutely sure what it is the funding body supports, and whether your intended project comes within that remit. In your correspondence with the funding body, state precisely what it is you intend to do. Be clear about your resources, your timetable, your goals, the results of your project and the means of dissemination of its results, and state exactly the value of your project in terms of its contribution to research or otherwise (especially, for example, if it has an economic value). Do not overestimate – remember that experts will probably be inspecting your application. Do not underestimate – you will not help yourself by setting unrealistic tasks or deadlines. Communicate coherently and in detail about your project, but avoid jargon, as specialists and non-specialists alike must be able to understand the purpose and function of your research. Aid the coherence of your application by giving it a short title, including an appropriate summary of the project, and also by getting a non-specialist as well as a specialist to read it through before you submit it to the awarding body. Make sure you are giving the information required by this particular funding body. If the funding body is asking for brief details, supply only as much as is required. Do not recycle applications made elsewhere, but produce one specifically aimed at the funding body to which you are applying.

d) Prepare well

Give yourself plenty of time to make an application. Make sure you have got all the details you need from the funding body before you apply, and digest them fully. Make sure you know everything you need to know about the funding body, and, if possible, speak to them about the project and its suitability beforehand. Check the deadline for submission and make sure you will be able to achieve it with time to spare. Think in detail about the project and what it will involve. Cost the project realistically, thinking about each area in turn (for example travel, subsistence, conferences, equipment, recurrent costs, data processing, secretarial work, publication costs, salaries and so on). Look at the possible limitations set by the funding body with regard to transferring money from person to person as well as from year to year. Think carefully about your proposed methodology, and whether or not it is suitable to the research project, as well as the funding body. With regard to all deadlines, both for submission and completion, think realistically – inexperienced researchers should talk to more experienced colleagues in order to avoid underestimating the work involved.

e) Present well

Presentation is extremely important at a time when the standard of submissions is generally very high. Apart from communicating well (see above), avoid cold-calling funding bodies. If possible, avoid using the telephone as a first means of enquiry – letters or emails always allow you to focus your mind on the submission and give the funding body time to respond accurately (phone conversations can be much more hit-and-miss). Do not send applications without prior communications – this does not leave a good impression. When you do send in your application, make sure it is of the highest quality, not only in terms of content, but style. Ensure your referees are the best you can get for your subject, know the value of your research and have good reputations themselves; and, if possible, impress upon them the need for timely, presentable submissions.

4   Useful addresses and further links

a) Research Councils:

The Arts and Humanities Research Council
Polaris House
North Star Avenue
Swindon
SN2 1FL
Tel 01793 41 6000
Web www.ahrc.ac.uk

The British Academy
10 Carlton House Terrace
London
SW1Y 5AH
Tel 020 7969 5200
Fax 020 6969 5300
Web www.britac.ac.uk

Economic and Social Research Council (ESRC)
Polaris House
North Star Avenue
Swindon
SN2 1UJ

Tel 01793 413000
Fax 01793 413001
Web www.esrc.ac.uk

Department of Education Northern Ireland
Rathgael House
43 Balloo Road
Bangor
Co Down
BT19 7PR
Tel 028 9127 9279
Fax 028 9127 9100
Web www.deni.gov.uk

Isle of Man Department of Education
Hamilton House
Peel Road
Douglas
Isle of Man
IM1 5EZ
Tel 01624 685820
Web www.gov.im/education/

Scottish Higher Education Funding Council
Apex House
97 Haymarket Terrace
Edinburgh
EH12 5HD
Tel 0131 313 6500
Fax 0131 313 6501
Web www.sfc.ac.uk

Higher Education Funding Council for Wales
Linden Court
Ilex Close
Llanishen
Cardiff
CF14 5DZ
Tel 029 2076 1861
Fax 029 2076 3163
Web www.hefcw.ac.uk

b) Websites

As with many areas of historical research activity, the web has revolutionised the process of reading about, hunting down, and applying for financial sources. It cannot be underlined enough that a couple of hours spent investigating different funding-related sites will more than repay itself. There is often a greater number of relevant sites than expected, and the web can make us aware of routes of support we may not have come across otherwise, and stimulate thoughts about possible alternatives in our funding search.

No definitive taxonomy of funding websites can be given here. However, some of the main types likely to be of use include: sites belonging to funding bodies, which can give full information about an organisation's aims, its stipulations for application and often the application form itself; sites which specifically exist to disseminate information on funding – there has been a notable rise in the number and quality of websites produced by universities themselves listing funding sources; and sites – commercial and non-commercial – which act as agents in the search for funding, or are set up by governments to channel information on public funding. And, of course, there are the generic search engines such as Google. Typing a key term into a search engine will result in pages of information and links. Some of this can be discarded as non-relevant. Much, however, will prove of great value, and you may be surprised by the alternative funding routes thrown up by such a search.

The following websites are particularly useful:

The application procedure

FinAid: www.finaid.org/scholarships/

Sites listing funding sources and links (general)

Community of Science: www.cos.com/cgi-bin/international/view/13/236/
University of Iowa Arts and Humanities Funding Sources: http://research.uiowa.edu/funding-and-development
Grants and Related Resources: http://staff.lib.msu.edu/harris23/grants/index.htm
The British Academy: http://www.britac.ac.uk/funding/index.cfm
GrantSelect: www.grantselect.com
National Association of Student Financial Aid Administrators: http://www.nasfaa.org/
Funding Sources for Individuals (University of Wisconsin): http://grants.library.wisc.edu/index.html
ResearchResearch: www.researchresearch.com
FinAid: www.finaid.org/otheraid/grants.phtml
Study Abroad: www.studyabroad.com

Funding sites dedicated to history

H-Net Funding Announcements: www2.h-net.msu.edu/announce/group.cgi?type=Funding&age=archived
Grants, Fellowships and Prizes – the American Historical Association: www.historians.org
Diplomatic History Resources Index: www.sarantakes.com/stuff-funding.html

Grants for Individuals – Michigan State University: http://staff.lib.msu.edu/
harris23/grants/3subject.htm
University of Essex – History: http://www.essex.ac.uk/history/prospective_
students/postgraduates/funding.aspx
Art History: www.nyu.edu/gsas/dept/fineart/html/chinese/grants.html

5　Errors, experiences and additions

Although every effort has been made to ensure the accuracy of the details
contained in the *Guide*, information has of necessity been restricted to
that which is relevant to historians. The conditions and details of funding
arrangements also undergo frequent changes with the passing of time.
In consequence, seekers and providers of funding may discover gaps or
inaccuracies in the *Guide*.

Also, in the course of the application process, readers of the *Guide* may have a
particular experience or gain information which they think would benefit others
in applying for funding.

Finally, those who are intending to fund history research in the next year or so
are particularly encouraged to contact the IHR in order to have their details
included.

In any of these cases, please feel free to contact either:

Professor John R Davis
School of Social Science
Kingston University
Penrhyn Road
Kingston upon Thames
Surrey
KT1 2EE
Tel 020 8547 2000 x2300
Email J.Davis@kingston.ac.uk

or:

SAS Publications
School of Advanced Study
University of London
Senate House
Malet Street
London
WC1E 7HU
Tel 020 7862 8688
Email sas.publications@sas.ac.uk

1   Conference grants

1   British Association for Japanese Studies Conference Support

Awarding body: British Association for Japanese Studies (BAJS)
Address: BAJS, University of Essex, Colchester CO4 3SQ
Tel: 01206 872543
Fax: 01206 873965
Email: bajs@bajs.org.uk
Web: www.bajs.org.uk
Contact: BAJS Secretariat
Award: Open to UK and Japanese nationals for conference and seminar attendance, max £250 per individual, check website for details
Objective: To help graduate students attend conferences and seminars on a subject relating to Japanese studies
Subject: Japanese studies

2   Buchan Lectures

Awarding body: Society of Antiquaries of Scotland
Address: Society of Antiquaries of Scotland, Royal Museum, Chambers St, Edinburgh EH1 1JF
Tel: 0131 247 4133
Fax: 0131 247 4163
Email: grants@socantscot.org
Web: www.socantscot.org
Contact: Director
Award: Open to local archaeological, antiquarian or similar societies to help fund a lecture, symposium or conference (a lecture supported by this fund is known as a Buchan Lecture), value max £300, including lecturer's fee, check website for deadline
Objective: To fund lectures in those parts of Scotland which are not at present served by the Society's meetings
Subject: Scottish themes

3   Economic History Society Initiatives and Conference Fund

Awarding body: Economic History Society
Address: Economic History Society, Department of Economic and Social History, University of Glasgow, Lilybank House, Bute Gardens, Glasgow G12 8QQ
Tel: 0141 330 4662
Fax: 0141 330 4889
Email: ehsocsec@arts.gla.ac.uk
Web: www.ehs.org.uk
Contact: Administrative Secretary
Award: Value up to £2,000, events should be advertised on the Society's website, closing dates 1 Nov, 1 Feb, 1 May, 1 Aug
Objective: To encourage otherwise unfunded workshops, special meetings and other interesting initiatives
Subject: Economic and social history

4   Royal Historical Society Conference Assistance

Awarding body: Royal Historical Society
Address: Royal Historical Society (RHS Conference Assistance), University College London, Gower St, London WC1E 6BT
Tel: 020 7387 7532
Fax: 020 7387 7532
Email: royalhistsoc@ucl.ac.uk
Web: www.royalhistoricalsociety.org
Contact: Administrative Secretary
Award: Limited assistance available for conference organisers, closing dates Nov, Apr
Objective: To aid the financing of small, specialised, historical conferences, especially where there is substantial involvement for junior researchers
Subject: History

5   Society for the Study of French History Conference Bursaries

Awarding body: Society for the Study of French History
Address: Society for the Study of French History, School of History and Archives, Newman Building, University College Dublin, Belfield, Dublin 4, Ireland
Tel: (00353) 1 716 8151
Email: sandy.wilkinson@ucd.ie
Web: www.frenchhistorysociety.ac.uk
Contact: Secretary
Award: Value up to £300, unlimited number of awards open to postgraduates registered for a degree, no deadline, applicants should be members of Society
Objective: To allow postgraduates to attend conferences and present papers related to research into French history

Subject: Any aspect of French history (including French colonial history)

6   Society for the Study of French History Conference Grants

Awarding body: Society for the Study of French History
Address: Society for the Study of French History, School of History and Archives, Newman Building, University College Dublin, Belfield, Dublin 4, Ireland
Tel: (00353) 1 716 8151
Email: sandy.wilkinson@ucd.ie
Web: www.frenchhistorysociety.ac.uk
Contact: Secretary
Award: Value up to £500, unlimited number of awards, no deadline
Objective: To assist established academics and postgraduates in Irish or British universities to mount conferences related to French history
Subject: Any aspect of French history (including French colonial history) or international history conferences with a substantial French component

7   Society of Antiquaries of Scotland Bursaries for Young Fellows Attending Conferences

Awarding body: Society of Antiquaries of Scotland
Address: Society of Antiquaries of Scotland, Royal Museum, Chambers St, Edinburgh EH1 1JF
Tel: 0131 247 4133
Fax: 0131 247 4163
Email: grants@socantscot.org
Web: www.socantscot.org
Contact: Research Committee
Award: Value max £300, open to those under 25 years of age, who should not have held a full-time salaried post for more than 5 years, closing date 30 Nov
Objective: To enable young Fellows of the Society to give papers on Scottish themes at conferences of international standing within Britain or abroad
Subject: Scottish themes

2 Fieldwork and heritage

8 American Schools of Oriental Research Excavation Fellowships

Awarding body: American Schools of Oriental Research (ASOR) (USA)
Address: ASOR, Boston University, 656 Beacon St, 5th Floor, Boston, MA 02215-2010, USA
Tel: (001) 617 353 6570
Fax: (001) 617 353 6575
Email: asor@bu.edu
Web: www.asor.org
Award: Various fellowships offered, up to about US$1,000, funding available for undergraduates, postgraduates and postdoctoral scholars
Objective: To allow individuals to participate in excavations in the Eastern Mediterranean
Subject: Near Eastern archaeology

9 American Schools of Oriental Research Mesopotamian Fellowship

Awarding body: American Schools of Oriental Research (ASOR) (USA)
Address: ASOR, Boston University, 656 Beacon St, 5th Floor, Boston, MA 02215, USA
Tel: (001) 617 353 6570
Fax: (001) 617 353 6575
Email: asor@bu.edu
Web: www.asor.org
Contact: Mesopotamian Fellowship
Award: One offered annually, value US$9,000, for 3–12 months, closing date 1 Dec
Objective: To support field or museum research in ancient Mesopotamian civilisation by graduate or postdoctoral scholars
Subject: Mesopotamian civilisation

10 Architectural Heritage Fund Grants and Low-Interest Loans

Awarding body: Architectural Heritage Fund
Address: The Architectural Heritage Fund, Alhambra House, 27–31 Charing Cross Rd, London WC2H 0AU
Tel: 020 7925 0199
Email: ahf@ahfund.org.uk
Web: www.ahfund.org.uk
Award: Open to building preservation trusts, other charities and eligible organisations, loan and grant applications considered quarterly
Objective: For projects to restore historic buildings
Subject: Architectural heritage

11 British School at Athens Fieldwork Bursary

Awarding body: British School at Athens (BSA) (Greece)
Address: BSA, 52 Souedias, 10676 Athens, Greece
Tel: (0030) 211 1022 800
Fax: (0030) 211 1022 803
Email: assistant.director@bsa.ac.uk
Web: www.bsa.ac.uk
Contact: Assistant Director
Award: Value max £200, open to students registered at UK universities, preference may be given to those at postgraduate level, closing date 1 Apr
Objective: To allow students to participate in BSA Hellenic projects
Subject: Hellenic archaeology and history

12   Challenge Funding

Awarding body: Council for British Archaeology (CBA)
Address: CBA, St Mary's House, 66 Bootham, York Y030 7BZ
Tel: 01904 671417
Fax: 01904 671384
Email: admin@britarch.ac.uk
Web: www.archaeologyuk.org/challenge-funding
Award: Up to £750 for groups, societies or individuals for projects involving original research into the historic environment
Objective: Challenge Funding is intended to encourage independent, voluntary effort in making original contributions to the study and care of Britain's historic environment, funds cannot be used to cover salary or publication costs, or to help writing theses or dissertations, available to projects in England and Wales
Subject: Archaeology

13   Essex Heritage Trust Grants

Awarding body: Essex Heritage Trust
Address: Essex Heritage Trust, Cressing Temple, Braintree, Essex CM77 8PD
Tel: 01376 585794
Fax: 01376 585794
Email: EHT@dsl.pipex.com
Web: www.essexheritagetrust.co.uk
Contact: Mrs Sharon Hill
Award: One-off grants awarded 3 times a year to projects within the administrative county of Essex, seeking aid
Objective: To support the preservation of land, buildings, objects or records significant to the county of Essex, including funding for publications significant to the county's heritage
Subject: Essex history

14   Heritage Grants

Awarding body: Heritage Lottery Fund
Address: Heritage Lottery Fund, 7 Holbein Pl, London SW1W 8NR
Tel: 020 7591 6000
Fax: 020 7591 6001
Email: enquire@hlf.org.uk
Web: www.hlf.org.uk
Award: Grants over £100,000 to not-for-profit organisations for projects related to heritage in the UK, information about application deadlines can be found on the HLF website
Objective: To fund projects that make a lasting difference for heritage, people and communities
Subject: Heritage

15   Margaret and Tom Jones Fund

Awarding body: Society of Antiquaries of London
Address: Society of Antiquaries of London, Burlington House, Piccadilly, London W1J 0BE
Tel: 020 7479 7080
Fax: 020 7287 6967
Email: hcockle@sal.org.uk
Web: www.sal.org.uk/grants/themargaretandtom/
Contact: Research Committee
Award: Value up to £10,500, closing date 15 Jan
Objective: For British landscape archaeology of the Neolithic to post-medieval periods (priority will be given to applications related to the excavations at Mucking, Essex, 1965–78) and for the methodology for the field investigation, excavation or analysis of large sites or landscapes
Subject: Landscape archaeology and methodology

16   Our Heritage

Awarding body: Heritage Lottery Fund
Address: Heritage Lottery Fund, 7
Holbein Pl, London SW1W 8NR
Tel: 020 7591 6000
Fax: 020 7591 6001
Email: enquire@hlf.org.uk
Web: www.hlf.org.uk
Award: Grants from £10,000–
£100,000 to not-for-profit
organisations and private owners
of heritage for projects related to
heritage in the UK, no deadline
Objective: To fund projects that make
a lasting difference for heritage,
people and communities
Subject: Heritage

17   Robert Kiln Charitable Trust Grants

Awarding body: Robert Kiln Charitable
Trust
Address: Robert Kiln Charitable Trust,
15a Bull Plain, Hertford, Herts SG14
1DX
Email: robertkilntrust@btconnect.com
Contact: Mrs S Howell, Trust
Administrator
Award: For general charitable
purposes with a preference for small
local organisations, value £25–£2,500
(usually £500), will support new
projects particularly from small local
organisations but the emphasis is on
long-term relationships, enclose SAE
with application
Objective: To support archaeology,
local charities and environmental
conservation
Subject: Archaeology and history, with
a special interest in Hertfordshire and
Bedfordshire

18   Sharing Heritage

Awarding body: Heritage Lottery Fund
Address: Heritage Lottery Fund, 7
Holbein Pl, London SW1W 8NR
Tel: 020 7591 6000
Fax: 020 7591 6001
Email: enquire@hlf.org.uk
Web: www.hlf.org.uk
Award: Grants from £3,000–£10,000
to not-for-profit organisations for
projects related to heritage in the UK
that will last no more than one year,
no deadline
Objective: To fund projects that make
a lasting difference for heritage,
people and communities
Subject: Heritage

19   Tessa and Mortimer Wheeler Memorial Fund

Awarding body: Society of Antiquaries
of London
Address: Society of Antiquaries of
London, Burlington House, Piccadilly,
London W1J 0BE
Tel: 020 7479 7080
Fax: 020 7287 6967
Email: hcockle@sal.org.uk
Web: www.sal.org.uk/grants/
tessaandmortimer/
Contact: Research Committee
Award: Value up to £500, available
to undergraduates or first-year
postgraduates, closing date 15 Jan
Objective: To assist students of
archaeology to gain experience in the
field in the UK and abroad
Subject: Archaeology

3 Guest fellowships and relocation

20 AAUW International Fellowships

Awarding body: American Association of University Women (AAUW) (USA)
Address: AAUW Educational Foundation, c/o Customer Service Center, ACT Inc, PO Box 4030, Iowa City, IA 52243-4030, USA
Tel: (001) 319 337 1716 ext 60
Email: aauw@act.org
Web: www.aauw.org
Award: US$18,000 for Master's/Professional Fellowship; US$20,000 for Doctoral Fellowship; US$30,000 for Postdoctoral Fellowship, apply from 1 Aug, closing date 1 Dec
Objective: For full-time study or research, open to women who are not US citizens or permanent residents
Subject: Any

21 A G Leventis Fellowship in Hellenic Studies

Awarding body: British School at Athens (BSA) (Greece)
Address: BSA, 52 Souedias, 106 76 Athens, Greece
Tel: (0030) 211 1022 800
Fax: (0030) 211 1022 803
Email: school.administrator@bsa.ac.uk
Web: www.bsa.ac.uk
Contact: School Administrator
Award: Salary for up to 3 years, annual return travel home up to £300, research expenses up to £1,500, fellow must have an affiliation with a UK university, be fluent in Greek and English and have satisfied all doctorate requirements no more than 5 years and at least 3 months before taking up the post which will be advertised on website when open
Objective: To support research into the anthropology, archaeology, architecture, arts, history, religion of Greece and Cyprus and related areas
Subject: To strengthen the School's relations with Greece and Cyprus

22 Albin Salton Research Fellowship

Awarding body: Warburg Institute – University of London
Address: Warburg Institute, University of London, Woburn Sq, London WC1H 0AB
Tel: 020 7862 8949
Fax: 020 7862 8955
Email: warburg@sas.ac.uk
Web: http://warburg.sas.ac.uk/fellowships/
Contact: Institute Manager
Award: One offered, value up to £2,500 for 2 months, open to those with at least a year's doctoral research or, if postdoctoral, must normally have been awarded their doctorate within the preceding 5 years, closing date 30 Nov
Objective: To enable a younger scholar to spend 2 months at the Warburg Institute pursuing research in cultural contacts between Europe, the East and the New World in the 14th–17th centuries, and to promote the understanding of those elements of cultural and intellectual history which led to a new world-view
Subject: Cultural contacts between Europe, the East and the New World in the late medieval, Renaissance and early modern periods

23 Albright Fellowships

Awarding body: W F Albright Institute of Archaeological Research (USA)
Address: Albright Fellowship Committee, Department of Art and Art History, Providence College, Providence, RI 02918, USA
Tel: (001) 401 865 1789
Fax: (001) 401 865 2410
Email: jbranham@providence.edu
Web: www.aiar.org/fellowships.html
Contact: Dr Joan R Branham, Chair, Albright Fellowship Committee
Award: Thirty-two fellowships awarded annually, up to a total of US$325,000 per year, open to students and scholars of the Near East from prehistory to the early Islamic period, awards include stipend and residency at Albright Institute
Objective: For research at the Institute
Subject: Ancient Near Eastern studies, including the fields of archaeology, anthropology, art history, Bible, epigraphy, historical geography, history, language, literature, philology and religion and related disciplines, from prehistory to the early Islamic period

24 Alfred D Chandler Jr International Visiting Scholars

Awarding body: Harvard Business School (USA)
Address: Harvard Business School, Connell 301A, Boston, MA 02163, USA
Email: wfriedman@hbs.edu
Web: www.hbs.edu
Contact: Walter A Friedman
Award: One available annually, value US$7,000, open to established scholars of business history from outside the US, duration 2–6 months, includes access to the School's facilities, closing date 15 Sept
Objective: To allow established scholars in business history to spend a period of time in residence at Harvard Business School
Subject: Business history

25 American School of Classical Studies at Athens Fellowships

Awarding body: American School of Classical Studies at Athens (ASCSA) (Greece)
Address: ASCSA, Odhós Souidías 54, Athens GR-10676, Greece
Tel: (0030) 210 72 36313
Fax: (0030) 210 72 50584
Email: ascsa@ascsa.edu.gr
Web: www.ascsa.edu.gr
Award: Number of fellowships offered, value US$1,875–US$30,000, plus board and lodging, generally open to students and scholars from the US and Canada, check website for details
Objective: For study at the School
Subject: Archaeology, archaeological sciences, history, art history and classical studies

26 Andrew W Mellon Postdoctoral Fellowships in the Humanities

Awarding body: Penn Humanities Forum – University of Pennsylvania (USA)
Address: Penn Humanities Forum, University of Pennsylvania, 3619 Locust Walk, Philadelphia, PA 19104-6213, USA
Tel: (001) 215 898 8220
Email: phf@sas.upenn.edu
Web: http://humanities.sas.upenn.edu/
Contact: Jennifer Conway, Associate Director
Award: Five fellowships offered annually, value US$46,500, plus health insurance and a US$2,500 research fund, for 1 year, for those without tenure no more than 8 years out of the PhD, annual CFA posted late May on Forum's website, closing date 15 Oct
Objective: For research at Penn Humanities Forum, University of Pennsylvania, with fellows expected to teach one undergraduate course during their fellowship year
Subject: Topic set annually by the Forum, topic for 2014–15 is 'Colour'; for 2015–16 'Sex'

27 Anglo-Danish Scholarship Awards

Awarding body: Anglo-Danish Society (registered charity no. 313202)
Address: Anglo-Danish Society, 6 Keats Ave, Littleover, Derby DE23 4ED
Tel: 01332 513932
Email: scholarships@anglo-danishsociety.org.uk
Web: www.anglo-danishsociety.org.uk
Contact: Mrs Margit Staehr, Administrator
Award: Number varies, open to postgraduates with a first degree from a Danish university who have started or are registered for a higher degree in the UK, or postgraduates with a first degree from a British university who have started or are registered for a higher degree in Denmark, min value £1,500 per grant, closing date 1 Mar
Objective: To assist Danish postgraduates who wish to study within a department of a university in the UK or British postgraduates who wish to study within a department of a university in Denmark
Subject: Non subject-specific, for exceptions see website

28 ARC Early Career Researcher Visiting Program

Awarding body: ARC Centre of Excellence in the History of Emotions (Europe 1100–1800) (Australia)
Address: Faculty of Arts, University of Western Australia, M201/35 Stirling Highway, Crawley 6009 WA, Australia
Email: philippa.maddern@uwa.edu.au
Web: www.historyofemotions.org.au/get-involved/ecr-visitors.aspx
Contact: Professor Philippa Maddern, Centre Director
Award: Return airfare to Australia, accommodation, travel costs plus daily allowance for period of 2 months, open to scholars who received the PhD between 2004 and 2012 who are based outside Australia, closing date Aug
Objective: To fund early career researchers to work with members of the Centre on a research programme of their choice
Subject: History of emotions

29   Association of Rhodes Scholars in Australia Scholarship

Awarding body: Association of Rhodes Scholars in Australia (Australia)
Address: Association of Rhodes Scholars in Australia Scholarship Committee, Melbourne Research Office, University of Melbourne, Victoria 3010, Australia
Tel: (0061) 3 8344 2058
Fax: (0061) 3 9347 6739
Email: aliceb@unimelb.edu.au
Web: www.research.unimelb.edu.au/rgc/grants/find/schemes/uom/rhodes_scholars/
Contact: Senior Grants Officer
Award: Offered in alternate years, value up to A$20,000, for travel and living expenses, for 6–12 months in Australia, for closing date see website
Objective: To enable a visit by postgraduate research candidates enrolled at a Commonwealth university outside Australia or New Zealand to work in their field of research and to make contact with Australian experts
Subject: Any subject

30   Australian Bicentennial Scholarships and Fellowships

Awarding body: Menzies Centre for Australian Studies
Address: Menzies Centre for Australian Studies, King's College London, Strand, London WC2R 2LS
Tel: 020 7848 1079
Fax: 020 7848 2052
Email: menzies.centre@kcl.ac.uk
Web: www.kcl.ac.uk/menzies/
Contact: Secretary
Award: Various scholarships and/or fellowships offered annually, value up to £4,000, tenable at any approved Australian tertiary institution, open to UK postgraduates/postdoctoral, also available for Australian scholars wishing to come to the UK, closing date end Mar
Objective: For scholarship and intellectual links and understanding between Australia and the UK
Subject: Any subject

31   Balsdon Fellowship

Awarding body: British School at Rome (BSR)
Address: BSR, British Academy, 10 Carlton House Terrace, London SW1Y 5AH
Tel: 020 7969 5202
Fax: 020 7969 5401
Email: bsr@britac.ac.uk
Web: www.bsr.ac.uk
Contact: Gill Clark, BSR London Office
Award: One offered annually, includes board and lodging for 3 months, open to established senior scholars, closing date mid Jan
Objective: To allow scholars engaged in research to spend a period of time in Rome
Subject: Archaeology, art history, history, society and culture of Italy

32 Bibliographic Association of America Fellowships

Awarding body: Bibliographic Association of America (USA)
Address: Bibliographical Society of America, PO Box 1537, Lenox Hill Station, New York, NY 10021, USA
Tel: (001) 212 452 2710
Email: fellowships@bibsocamer.org
Web: www.bibsocamer.org
Contact: Society Secretary
Award: Several short-term fellowships (1–2 months), stipend of up to US$3,000, check website for details, closing date 15 Dec
Objective: To support bibliographical inquiry as well as research in the history of the book trades and in publishing history
Subject: Bibliographical history, history of the book trades, publishing history

33 Brian Hewson Crawford Fellowship

Awarding body: Warburg Institute – University of London
Address: Warburg Institute, University of London, Woburn Sq, London WC1H 0AB
Tel: 020 7862 8949
Fax: 020 7862 8955
Email: warburg@sas.ac.uk
Web: http://warburg.sas.ac.uk/fellowships/
Contact: Institute Manager
Award: One offered, value up to £2,500 for 2 months, open to European scholars other than of British nationality, open to those with at least 1 year's doctoral research, must normally have been awarded their doctorate within the previous 5 years, closing date 30 Nov
Objective: To promote research
Subject: Any aspect of the classical tradition

34 British Institute at Ankara Research Scholarship

Awarding body: British Institute at Ankara (BIAA)
Address: BIAA, 10 Carlton House Terrace, London SW1Y 5AH
Tel: 020 7969 5204
Fax: 020 7969 5401
Email: biaa@britac.ac.uk
Web: www.biaa.ac.uk
Contact: Claire McCafferty
Award: Value £800 per month, BIAA will pay cost of 1 return flight between Turkey and UK, 7 months based at Institute in Ankara, see website for deadlines
Objective: For scholar to work on BIAA electronic archives and own research
Subject: Focus on Turkey and/ or Black Sea, any discipline in humanities/social sciences

35 British School at Athens Early Career Fellowships

Awarding body: British School at Athens (BSA) (Greece)
Address: BSA, 52 Souedias, 106 76 Athens, Greece
Tel: (0030) 211 1022 800
Fax: (0030) 211 1022 803
Email: school.administrator@bsa.ac.uk
Web: www.bsa.ac.uk
Contact: School Administrator
Award: Non-stipendiary research fellowship in Greece, return airfare and accommodation, up to 3 months, fellows are expected to hold an informal seminar
Objective: To enable young scholars in post to spend a period of research in Greece
Subject: Any branch of the arts or sciences related to Greece

36   British School at Athens Visiting Fellowships

Awarding body: British School at Athens (BSA) (Greece)
Address: BSA, 52 Souedias, 106 76 Athens, Greece
Tel: (0030) 211 1022 800
Fax: (0030) 211 1022 803
Email: school.administrator@bsa.ac.uk
Web: www.bsa.ac.uk
Contact: School Administrator
Award: Non-stipendiary research fellowship in Greece, return airfare and accommodation, up to 3 months, fellows are expected to give a public lecture and hold an informal seminar
Objective: To allow research at the BSA
Subject: Any aspect of the history and archaeology of Greece

37   British School at Rome – Rome Awards

Awarding body: British School at Rome (BSR)
Address: BSR, British Academy, 10 Carlton House Terrace, London SW1Y 5AH
Tel: 020 7969 5202
Fax: 020 7969 5401
Email: bsr@britac.ac.uk
Web: www.bsr.ac.uk
Contact: BSR London Office
Award: Number varies, value £150 per month plus £180 travel, with board and lodging, normally for 3 months, postgraduate and early postdoctoral, closing date mid Jan
Objective: To allow scholars engaged in research to spend a period of time in Rome
Subject: Archaeology, art history, history, society and culture of Italy

38   Carl Albert Congressional Research and Studies Center Visiting Scholars Program

Awarding body: Carl Albert Congressional Research and Studies Center (USA)
Address: Carl Albert Center, 630 Parrington Oval, Room 101, University of Oklahoma, Norman, OK 73019, USA
Tel: (001) 405 325 5835
Fax: (001) 405 325 6419
Email: channeman@ou.edu
Web: www.ou.edu/special/albertctr.edu
Contact: Archivist
Award: Value US$500–US$1,000 for travel and lodging, mostly postgraduate and postdoctoral, applications accepted at any time
Objective: To support research by providing financial assistance to researchers working at the Center's archives
Subject: History, political science and other fields

39 Center for Advanced Holocaust Studies Fellowships

Awarding body: Center for Advanced Holocaust Studies – United States Holocaust Memorial Museum (USHMM) (USA)
Address: Center for Advanced Holocaust Studies, USHMM, 100 Raoul Wallenberg Pl, SW Washington, DC 20024-2126, USA
Tel: (001) 202 314 7289
Fax: (001) 202 479 9726
Email: visiting_scholars@ushmm.org
Web: www.ushmm.org/research/center/
Contact: Program Co-ordinator, Visiting Scholars Division
Award: Variable number awarded at the discretion of the Center, up to US$3,500 per month for 3–8 months in residence at the Museum, open to pre- and postdoctoral, and senior scholars, closing date in Nov
Objective: To support research and writing about the Holocaust and in genocide studies
Subject: Holocaust history and genocide studies

40 CIMO Fellowships

Awarding body: Centre for International Mobility (CIMO) (Finland)
Address: CIMO, PO Box 343 (Hakaniemenkatu 2), FI-00531 Helsinki, Finland
Tel: (00358) 206 90 501
Email: cimointo@cimo.fi
Web: www.studyinfinland.fi
Award: Duration 3–12 months, monthly allowance of €900–€1,200, application is through the Finnish host university and should be made at least 5 months before the intended scholarship period, for doctoral students only

Objective: To allow postgraduate scholars to study in Finnish universities
Subject: Any subject

41 Clark-Huntington Joint Bibliographical Fellowship

Awarding body: UCLA Center for 17th- and 18th-Century Studies (USA)
Address: Center for 17th- and 18th-Century Studies, 310 Royce Hall, UCLA, Los Angeles, CA 90095-1404, USA
Tel: (001) 310 206 8552
Fax: (001) 310 206 8577
Email: gwcloud@humnet.ucla.edu
Web: www.c1718cs.ucla.edu
Contact: Dr Gerald Cloud
Award: Value US$5,500 for 2 months in residence, open to postdoctoral candidates, closing date 1 Feb
Objective: To support bibliographical research in early modern British literature and history
Subject: British literature and history

42   Columbia Society of Fellows in the Humanities Postdoctoral Fellowships

Awarding body: Columbia University Society of Fellows in the Humanities (USA)
Address: Society of Fellows in the Humanities, Heyman Center, Mail Code 5700, Columbia University, 2960 Broadway, New York, NY 10027, USA
Email: sof-fellows@columbia.edu
Web: www.columbia.edu/cu/societyoffellows/
Contact: Director
Award: Value US$61,000, half for independent research and half for teaching in the undergraduate programme, plus US$5,000 to support research, closing date 1 Oct
Objective: To support research and teaching in the humanities
Subject: Humanities

43   Commonwealth Scholarship and Fellowship Plan

Awarding body: Association of Commonwealth Universities (ACU)
Address: Commonwealth Scholarship Commission in the UK, ACU, Woburn House, 20–24 Tavistock Square, London WC1H 9HF
Tel: 020 7380 6700
Fax: 020 7387 2655
Web: www.csfp-online.org
Contact: Executive Secretary, Human Capacity Development
Award: Scholarships and fellowships, mainly at postgraduate level, offered to citizens of Commonwealth countries by other Commonwealth governments
Objective: Established in 1959, it is a mechanism of pan-Commonwealth exchange, with participation based on a series of bilateral arrangements between home and host countries, participation of each country organised by a national nominating agency responsible for advertising awards applicable to their own country and making nominations to host countries
Subject: Unrestricted

44   Council for British Research in the Levant Visiting Research Fellowships and Scholarships

Awarding body: Council for British Research in the Levant (CBRL)
Address: CBRL, c/o British Academy, 10 Carlton House Terrace, London SW1Y 5AH
Tel: 020 7969 5296
Fax: 020 7969 5401
Email: cbrl@britac.ac.uk
Web: www.cbrl.org.uk
Award: Number varies, offered annually, closing date mid Jan
Objective: Fellowships enable postdoctoral researchers to spend 3, 6 or 12 months at one of the CBRL's overseas institutes to conduct research, develop contacts, give lectures, write up project results or work on publications dervied from their theses, visiting scholarships allow students conducting doctoral research to spend 6 or 12 months at one of the CBRL's overseas institutes to conduct research, develop contacts and write up research
Subject: Humanities and social science subjects including archaeology and historical studies relating to countries of the Levant

45   Craig Hugh Smyth Visiting Fellowship

Awarding body: Villa I Tatti (Italy)
Address: Fellowship Application Office, Villa I Tatti, Via di Vincigliata 26, 50135 Firenze, Italy
Tel: (0039) 055 603 251
Email: applications@itatti.harvard.edu
Web: www.itatti.harvard.edu
Award: Up to US$5,000 per month for 3 months' stay at the Center
Objective: To enable scholars who do not have the benefit of sabbatical leave to carry out research
Subject: Any field of Italian Renaissance studies: history (including science and philosophy), art history, literature and music

46   Daiwa Scholarships

Awarding body: Daiwa Anglo-Japanese Foundation
Address: Daiwa Anglo-Japanese Foundation, Japan House, 13/14 Cornwall Terrace, London NW1 4QP
Tel: 020 7486 4348
Fax: 020 7486 2914
Email: scholarships@dajf.org.uk
Web: www.dajf.org.uk/scholarships/general-information/
Award: Nineteen-month programme of language study, homestay and work placement in Japan, all costs covered, applicants must be UK citizens aged 20–35, closing date first Thursday in Dec
Objective: To offer future leaders from any discipline the opportunity to acquire a thorough knowledge of written and spoken Japanese and of Japanese life and culture
Subject: Any (other than Japanese)

47   David Bruce Centre Fellowships

Awarding body: David Bruce Centre for American Studies – Keele University
Address: David Bruce Centre for American Studies, Research Institute for the Humanities, Claus Moser Research Centre, Room CM0.25, Keele University, Keele ST5 5BG
Tel: 01782 734577
Email: brucecentre@keele.ac.uk
Web: www.keele.ac.uk/depts/as/Dbruce/bruce.htm
Contact: Tracey Wood, David Bruce Centre Administrator
Award: Provides office space and facilities plus up to £500 towards research travel and conference participation for visiting scholars, usually from the US, for between 2 weeks and a semester, closing dates 1 Dec, 1 Mar, 1 June, 1 Sep
Objective: To allow scholars to pursue research, but fellows are expected to contribute to the Bruce Centre seminar series and participate in teaching
Subject: United States studies

48   David Bruce Centre Visiting European Fellowships

Awarding body: David Bruce Centre for American Studies – Keele University
Address: David Bruce Centre for American Studies, Research Institute for the Humanities, Claus Moser Research Centre, Room CM0.25, Keele University, Keele ST5 5BG
Tel: 01782 734577
Email: brucecentre@keele.ac.uk
Web: www.keele.ac.uk/depts/as/Dbruce/bruce.htm
Contact: Tracey Wood, David Bruce Centre Administrator
Award: Covers travel and accommodation for visiting scholars from continental Europe for a week-long stay at Keele, also provides office space and facilities, closing dates 1 Dec, 1 Mar, 1 June, 1 Sep
Objective: To allow scholars to pursue research, but fellows are expected to contribute to the Bruce Centre seminar series and participate in teaching
Subject: United States studies

49   Everett Helm Visiting Fellowships

Awarding body: Lilly Library, Indiana University (USA)
Address: The Lilly Library, Indiana University Libraries, 1200 E 7th St, Bloomington, IN 47405, USA
Tel: (001) 812 855 2452
Fax: (001) 812 855 3143
Email: liblilly@indiana.edu
Web: www.indiana.edu/,liblilly/fellowships.shtml
Contact: Breon Mitchell, Director
Award: Up to US$1,500 in support of travel, living and/or research expenses, closing date 15 Apr

Objective: To support research and provide access to the collections of the Lilly Library
Subject: British, French and American literature and history; the literature of voyages and exploration, specifically the European expansion in the Americas; early printing; the Church; children's literature; music; film, radio and television; medicine, science and architecture; food and drink

50   Fellowship Program for Advanced Social Science Research on Japan

Awarding body: Japan-US Friendship Commission/National Endowment for the Humanities (NEH) (USA)
Address: NEH, Division of Research Programs, 1100 Pennsylvania Ave NW, Room 318, Washington, DC 20506, USA
Tel: (001) 202 606 8200
Email: fellowships@neh.gov
Web: www.neh.gov/grants/research/fellowships-advanced-social-science-research-japan.html
Contact: Division of Research Programs
Award: Fellowships of 6–12 months, stipend of US$4,200 per month, only US citizens or residents are eligible, research may take place in Japan or the US, closing date 1 May
Objective: To support research on the modern Japanese political economy, international relations and society, and on US-Japan relations
Subject: Anthropology, economics, geography, history, international relations, linguistics, political science, psychology, public administration and sociology

51   Fellowship Programs at Independent Research Institutions

Awarding body: National Endowment for the Humanities (NEH) (USA)
Address: NEH, Division of Research Programs, 1100 Pennsylvania Ave NW, Room 318, Washington, DC 20506, USA
Tel: (001) 202 606 8200
Email: fpiri@neh.gov
Web: www.neh.gov/grants/research/fellowship-programs-independent-research-institutions
Contact: Division of Research Programs
Award: Fellowships of 4–12 months, open to US citizens or residents, contact relevant organisation for details
Objective: To provide fellowship programmes for humanities scholars at independent centres for advanced study and international research organisations and to provide scholars with a collegial environment and access to resources that might not be available at their home institutions
Subject: Humanities

52   Folger Shakespeare Library Research Fellowships

Awarding body: Folger Shakespeare Library (USA)
Address: Folger Shakespeare Library, 201 East Capitol St SE, Washington, DC 20003, USA
Tel: (001) 202 544 4600
Fax: (001) 202 544 4623
Email: cbrobeck@folger.edu
Web: www.folger.edu/researchfellowships/
Contact: Carol Brobeck, Fellowships Administrator
Award: Limited number of long-term (6–9 months, stipend up to US$50,000) and short-term (1–3 months, stipend of US$2,500 per month) fellowships, closing dates 1 Nov (long-term fellowships), 1 Mar (short-term fellowships)
Objective: To encourage access to the library's exceptional collections and to encourage ongoing cross-disciplinary dialogue among scholars of the early modern period
Subject: Any humanities field supported by the Folger collections covering 1500–1800, English and continental histories of literature, science, political and religious thought, drama, etc

53   Foundation for the History of Women in Medicine Fellowships

Awarding body: Foundation for the History of Women in Medicine (USA)
Address: Foundation for the History of Women in Medicine, PO Box 543, Pottstown, PA 19464, USA
Tel: (001) 610 970 9143
Fax: (001) 610 970 7520
Email: fhwim@burkhartgroup.com
Web: www.fhwim.org/programs/fellowships.php
Award: One grant available, value US$5,000, for travel, lodging and research using the resources of the Countway Library, Harvard Medical School, and/or the Archives for Women in Medicine, check website for closing date
Objective: To support research projects
Subject: History of women in medicine

54   Frank Knox Fellowships at Harvard University

Awarding body: President and Fellows of Harvard College
Address: Frank Knox Memorial Fellowship, 3 Birdcage Walk, Westminster, London SW1H 9JJ
Tel: 020 7222 1151
Fax: 020 7222 7189
Email: anniet@kentrust.demon.co.uk
Web: www.frankknox.harvard.edu
Contact: Secretary, Frank Knox Fellowships
Award: Up to 6 offered annually, value at least US$26,000 (pre-tax) plus tuition fees and health insurance, for up to 2 consecutive years, postgraduate, for those who graduated in 2009 or later, closing date 23 Oct
Objective: To allow UK citizens to undertake postgraduate study at Harvard University
Subject: All subjects

55   Frederick Burkhardt Residential Fellowships for Recently Tenured Scholars

Awarding body: American Council of Learned Societies (ACLS) (USA)
Address: ACLS, 633 3rd Ave, 8C, New York, NY 10017-6795, USA
Tel: (001) 212 697 1505
Fax: (001) 212 949 8058
Email: grants@acls.org
Web: www.acls.org/grants/Default. aspx?id=480
Contact: Office of Fellowships and Grants
Award: Up to 9 offered, value US$75,000 for 1 year, open to recently tenured scholars in the humanities, tenable at one of 12 research centres, applicants must be employed at a US institution, closing date 26 Sept

Objective: To support ambitious projects to be carried out in residence at 9 major institutions
Subject: Subjects including anthropology, archaeology, history and art history, and social sciences employing humanistic approaches

56   Harvard Postdoctoral Fellowships in Japanese Studies

Awarding body: Edwin O Reischauer Institute of Japanese Studies – Harvard University (USA)
Address: Postdoctoral Fellowships, Reischauer Institute, 1737 Cambridge St, Cambridge, MA 02138, USA
Tel: (001) 617 495 3220
Fax: (001) 617 496 8083
Email: tgilman@fas.harvard.edu
Web: http://rijs.fas.harvard.edu/
Contact: Dr Theodore J Gilman
Award: A few 10-month fellowships available, stipend US$50,000, residence in Cambridge/Boston area and participation in Institute activities are required during the appointment, postdoctoral fellows will be expected to give a presentation at the Reischauer Institute's Japan Forum lecture series, teaching one undergraduate course for a semester is not required but certainly encouraged, deadline 2 Jan
Objective: To support exceptional candidates who have recently achieved the PhD (2009 or later) in turning their dissertations into publishable manuscripts
Subject: Japanese studies

57 Henry Moore Institute Research Fellowships

Awarding body: Henry Moore Institute
Address: Henry Moore Foundation, Dane Tree House, Perry Green, Herts SG10 6EE
Tel: 0113 246 7467
Email: kirstie@henry-moore.org
Web: www.henry-moore.org
Contact: Kirstie Gregory
Award: Small number of fellowships offered annually, check website for full details
Objective: To support research using the Institute's resources
Subject: Historic and contemporary sculpture

58 Hosei International Fund Foreign Scholars Fellowship

Awarding body: Hosei University (Japan)
Address: HIF Foreign Scholars Fellowship, International Centre, Hosei University, 2-17-1 Fujimi, Chiyoda-ku, Tokyo 102–8160, Japan
Tel: (0081) 3 3264 9404
Fax: (0081) 3 3264 4624
Email: hif@hosei.ac.jp
Web: www.hosei.ac.jp/ic/en/research/hif/
Contact: Co-ordinator
Award: Offered annually, duration 6–12 months, value up to ¥300,000 monthly plus travel subsidy, applicants must be enrolled in a doctoral plan, under 39 years of age and fluent in Japanese or English, closing date early June
Objective: To allow young scholars from outside Japan to carry out non-degree research programmes at Hosei University under the direction of and/or in co-operation with Hosei faculty and researchers

Subject: Humanities, social or natural sciences and engineering where deemed appropriate

59 Hugh Last Fellowship

Awarding body: British School at Rome (BSR)
Address: BSR, British Academy, 10 Carlton House Terrace, London SW1Y 5AH
Tel: 020 7969 5202
Fax: 020 7969 5401
Email: bsr@britac.ac.uk
Web: www.bsr.ac.uk
Contact: BSR London Office
Award: One offered annually, based in Rome, includes board and lodging for 3 months, open to established scholars, closing date mid Jan
Objective: To enable established scholars to collect research material concerning classical antiquity
Subject: Classical antiquity (excluding archaeological fieldwork and work on Roman Britain)

60   Hugh Le May Fellowship

Awarding body: Rhodes University (South Africa)
Address: Rhodes University, PO Box 94, Grahamstown 6140, South Africa
Tel: (0027) 46 603 8936
Fax: (0027) 46 622 8444
Email: research-admin@ru.ac.za
Web: www.ru.ac.za/research/funding/
Contact: Jaine Roberts, Director, Research Office
Award: One offered biennially, value small monthly stipend for 3–6 months, plus accommodation and return airfare, extendable, open to senior postdoctoral scholars with substantial research outputs, closing date 31 July
Objective: To support research at the University
Subject: Philosophy, classics, ancient, medieval or modern history, classical, biblical, medieval or modern languages, political theory, law

61   Humboldt Research Fellowship for Experienced Researchers

Awarding body: Alexander von Humboldt Foundation (Germany)
Address: Humboldt Foundation, Selection Department, Jean-Paul Strasse 12, D-53173, Bonn, Germany
Tel: (0049) 228 8330
Fax: (0049) 228 833 212
Email: info@avh.de
Web: www.humboldt-foundation.de
Award: Monthly fellowship rate of €3,150 plus research, travel and family allowances for 6–18 months, open to highly qualified, early stage researchers from abroad who completed their doctorate less than 12 years ago
Objective: To support long-term research stays in Germany for academics from outside Germany
Subject: Any subject

62   Huntington Research Awards

Awarding body: Huntington Library, Art Collections and Botanical Gardens (USA)
Address: Committee on Fellowships, The Huntington, 1151 Oxford Rd, San Marino, CA 91108, USA
Tel: (001) 626 405 2194
Email: cpowell@huntington.org
Web: www.huntington.org
Contact: Chair
Award: Value US$3,000 monthly stipend for 1–5 months, open to doctoral students at dissertation stage or those holding the PhD, closing date 15 Nov
Objective: To support study while in residence at the Huntington
Subject: British and American literature, history, art history and history of science and medicine

63 Italian Government Awards

Awarding body: Italian Cultural Institute
Address: Italian Cultural Institute, 39 Belgrave Sq, London SW1X 8NX
Tel: 020 7235 1461
Fax: 020 7235 4618
Email: icilondon@esteri.it
Web: www.icilondon.esteri.it
Contact: Scholarships Department
Award: Scholarships and bursaries offered for university graduates and PhD students, normally aged under 35, check website for closing dates
Objective: To enable study at Italian HEIs
Subject: Any subject, but mainly Italian language and literature, history of art

64 Jacob Rader Marcus Center Fellowship Program

Awarding body: Jacob Rader Marcus Center of the American Jewish Archives (USA)
Address: Jacob Rader Marcus Center of the American Jewish Archives, 3101 Clifton Ave, Cincinnati, OH 45220-2408, USA
Tel: (001) 513 487 3004 ext 304
Fax: (001) 513 221 7812
Email: AJA@huc.edu
Web: www.americanjewisharchives.org
Contact: Director of the Fellowship Program
Award: Up to 13 offered annually, covers transportation and living expenses, for 1 month's residence, open to postdoctoral researchers and those completing doctoral dissertations, closing date 8 Feb
Objective: For research and writing at the Center
Subject: Some area relating to the history of North American Jewry

65 Japanese Association of University Women (JAUW) International Fellowship

Awarding body: Japanese Association of University Women (JAUW) (Japan)
Address: JAUW International Fellowship Committee, 11-6-101 Samoncho, Shinjuku-ku, Tokyo 160-0017, Japan
Tel: (0081) 3 3358 2882
Email: jauw@jauw.org
Web: www.ifuw.org/fellowships/japan.shtml
Contact: Ms Kazuka Hirano, Chair
Award: Open to International Federation of University Women members undertaking research in Japan for at least 3 months, value ¥500,000–¥1,000,000 depending on length of stay and nature of the work, closing date 20 Apr
Objective: To promote international cultural exchange and mutual understanding
Subject: Any subject

66   Japanese Government (MEXT) Scholarships for Research Students

Awarding body: Japanese Ministry of Education, Culture, Sports, Science and Technology (MEXT)
Address: Embassy of Japan, 101–104 Piccadilly, London W1J 7JT
Tel: 020 7465 6583
Email: scholarship@ld.mofa.go.jp
Web: www.uk.emb-japan.go.jp
Contact: MEXT Postgraduate Scholarships
Award: Scholarships offered annually for 18 months–2 years, monthly allowance of ¥150,000 (sufficient to cover most normal expenses for a single person), return airfare to Japan, opportunity to carry out research at a Japanese university with the possibility of entering a taught degree, 6-month Japanese language course, health cover, open to graduates under the age of 35, applications for 2015–17 will be available in Apr 2014
Objective: To allow UK nationals to study at universities in Japan
Subject: Any subject as long as it is relevant to a grantee's field of expertise or previous study

67   Kennedy Memorial Trust Scholarships

Awarding body: Kennedy Memorial Trust
Address: Kennedy Memorial Trust, 3 Birdcage Walk, Westminster, London SW1H 9JJ
Tel: 020 7222 1151
Fax: 020 7222 7189
Email: anniet@kentrust.demon.co.uk
Web: www.kennedytrust.org.uk
Contact: Secretary, Kennedy Memorial Trust
Award: Ten offered annually, value at least US$24,500 to cover support, plus tuition fees and travelling expenses, tenable at Harvard University and MIT for 1 year, closing date 23 Oct
Objective: To allow a UK citizen who has spent 2 of the last 7 academic years at a UK university and who has graduated before applying for the award to undertake a postgraduate course of study in the USA
Subject: Any subject

68   Kenneth Lindsay Scholarship Trust Grants

Awarding body: Anglo-Israel Association
Address: Anglo Israel Association, Kenneth Lindsay Scholarship Trust, PO Box 47819, London NW11 7WD
Tel: 020 8458 1284
Fax: 020 8458 3484
Email: info@angloisraelassociation.com
Web: www.angloisraelassociation.com
Contact: Executive Director
Award: Grants of £500–£2,000 to enable students from Israel to advance their education at universities and institutions of higher learning in the UK, covers 1 year of study only, closing date 31 May
Objective: To encourage close collaboration between individuals of both countries
Subject: Any

69   Lemmermann Foundation Scholarships

Awarding body: Lemmermann Foundation (Italy)
Address: Fondazione Lemmermann, c/o Studio Romanelli, via Cosseria 5, 100192 Roma, Italy
Tel: (0039) 06321 17 46
Fax: (0039) 06322 17 88
Email: lemmermann@nexus.it
Web: www.nexus.it/lemmermann/
Contact: Scholarships Secretary
Award: Value €750 monthly, applicants should be attending a recognised university course and have a basic knowledge of Italian, closing date 15 Mar
Objective: To assist students who need to carry out research in Rome
Subject: Rome and Roman culture from the pre-Roman period to the present day, in the fields of archaeology, history, history of art, Italian, Latin, musicology, philosophy, philology and others

70   Leverhulme Trust Study Abroad Studentships

Awarding body: Leverhulme Trust
Address: Research Awards Advisory Committee, Leverhulme Trust, 1 Pemberton Row, London EC4A 3BG
Tel: 020 7042 9861
Fax: 020 7042 9889
Email: bkerr@leverhulme.ac.uk
Web: www.leverhulme.ac.uk
Contact: Bridget Kerr
Award: Approx 20 offered, value £17,000 pa, plus return airfare and possibility of further allowances, including £6,000 for a dependent partner, postgraduate and postdoctoral, closing date 13 Jan
Objective: To allow a period of advanced study or research at a centre of learning anywhere in the world except the UK or USA
Subject: Any subject

71   Mellon Fellowships in the Humanities

Awarding body: Institute of Historical Research (IHR) – University of London
Address: IHR, University of London, Senate House, Malet St, London WC1E 7HU
Tel: 020 7862 8740
Fax: 020 7862 8745
Email: james.lees@sas.ac.uk
Web: www.history.ac.uk
Contact: Fellowships Officer
Award: Five 1-year dissertation fellowships value US$25,000, 7 short-term pre-dissertation fellowships (not more than 2 months) value US$5,000, open to students registered for the PhD at a North American university, closing date mid Jan
Objective: To allow North American PhD students access to British archives
Subject: Humanities

72   Mellon Visiting Fellowship

Awarding body: Villa I Tatti (Italy)
Address: Fellowship Application
Office, Villa I Tatti, Via di Vincigliata
26, 50135 Florence, Italy
Tel: (0039) 055 603 251
Email: applications@itatti.harvard.edu
Web: www.itatti.harvard.edu
Award: Max stipend US$5,000 per
month, for periods of 3–6 months,
preference will be given to junior
scholars who teach or plan to teach in
Asia, Islamic countries, Latin America
and the Mediterranean basin, closing
date 1 Feb
Objective: To support and promote
Italian Renaissance studies in areas
that have been under-represented at
I Tatti
Subject: Any field of Italian
Renaissance studies: history
(including science and philosophy), art
history, literature and music

73   Mendel Fellowships

Awarding body: Lilly Library, Indiana
University (USA)
Address: The Lilly Library, Indiana
University Libraries, 1200 E 7th St,
Bloomington, IN 47405, USA
Tel: (001) 812 855 2452
Fax: (001) 812 855 3143
Email: liblilly@indiana.edu
Web: www.indiana.edu/,liblilly/
fellowships.shtml
Contact: Breon Mitchell, Director
Award: Stipend of up to US$40,000
for fellowship of up to a year, closing
dates 15 Apr
Objective: To support research in the
library's Bernardo Mendel collections
Subject: History of the Spanish
colonial Empire; Latin American
independence movements; European
expansion in the Americas; voyages,
travels and exploration; geography,

navigation and cartography; German
literature and history; and music,
including sheet music

74   The Metropolitan Museum of Art Fellowships

Awarding body: Metropolitan Museum
of Art (USA)
Address: Metropolitan Museum of Art,
1000 5th Ave, New York, NY 10028-
0198, USA
Email: education.grants@
metmuseum.org
Web: www.metmuseum.org/en/
research/internships-and-fellowships/
fellowships/
Contact: Marcie Karp
Award: Several programmes, number
varies, value US$32,000–$42,000 pa,
plus US$6,000 for travel, closing date
early Dec
Objective: To support study and
training related to the Museum's
collections
Subject: Art history, conservation or
related fields

75 National Humanities Center Fellowships

Awarding body: National Humanities Center (USA)
Address: Fellowship Program, National Humanities Center, 7 Alexander Drive, PO Box 12256, Research Triangle Park, NC 27709-2256, USA
Tel: (001) 919 549 0661
Fax: (001) 919 990 8535
Email: nhc@nationalhumanitiescenter.org
Web: http://nationalhumanitiescenter.org/
Contact: Fellowship Program
Award: Forty residential fellowships to a value of at least half salary plus travel expenses for fellows and their dependants, applicants must hold doctorate or equivalent scholarly credentials and will be expected to work at the Center, closing date mid Oct
Objective: To facilitate advanced scholarly research at the National Humanities Center
Subject: Humanities, individual fellowships are also available in some specific areas

76 Newton International Fellowships

Awarding body: Newton International Fellowships (Royal Society and British Academy)
Address: Newton International Fellowships, 6–9 Carlton House Terrace, London SW1Y 5AG
Tel: 020 7451 2559
Fax: 020 7930 2170
Email: info@newtonfellowships.org
Web: www.newtonfellowships.org
Award: Grant of £24,000 pa to cover subsistence and up to £8,000 pa to cover research expenses, plus a one-off relocation allowance of up to £2,000, with the possibility of follow-up funding of up to £6,000 pa for 10 years after, open to early-career researchers with non-UK citizenship and who are currently working outside the UK, closing date 4 Apr
Objective: To support early-career researchers and to encourage the development of a global pool of research leaders with ties to the UK
Subject: All subject areas of physical, natural and social sciences; social sciences, and the humanities covered by the Royal Society and the British Academy

77 Norwegian Research Council Yggdrasil Mobility Programme

Awarding body: Norwegian Research Council
Address: Norwegian Research Council, PO Box 2700, St Hanshaugen NO-0131, Oslo, Norway
Tel: (0047) 220 37000
Fax: (0047) 220 37001
Email: intstip@rcn.no
Web: www.rcn.no/is/
Contact:
Award: Open to applicants from 50 countries, value NOK12,500 per month (young PhD students) or NOK15,000 per month (those who have held PhDs for not more than 6 years) for up to 10 months, plus NOK10,000 settling-in expenses, closing date 16 Feb
Objective: To make Norway an attractive research destination for highly qualified international PhD students and younger researchers
Subject: Any subject

78 NWO Rubicon Scholarship

Awarding body: Netherlands Organisation for Scientific Research (NWO) (The Netherlands)
Address: NWO, P/O Box 93138, NL 2509 AC Den Haag, The Netherlands
Tel: (0031) 70 349 44 37
Email: rubicon@nwo.nl
Web: www.nwo.nl
Contact: Ms H R Varwijk
Award: Research fellowship of 1–2 years, tenable at an institution in the Netherlands or elsewhere, funding to cover accommodation, travel costs and research costs, open to postgraduates engaged in doctoral research or those who have been awarded a PhD in the last 12 months, closing dates 29 Nov, 3 Apr, 4 Sept
Objective: To encourage talented researchers to pursue a career in postdoctoral research and to attract international scholars to the Netherlands
Subject: All

79 Pantzer Senior Fellowship

Awarding body: Bibliographic Association of America (USA)
Address: Bibliographical Society of America, PO Box 1537, Lenox Hill Station, New York, NY 10021, USA
Email: bsa@bibsocamer.org
Web: www.bibsocamer.org
Contact: Executive Secretary
Award: Fellowship of 2–3 months, stipend US$6,000, closing date 1 Dec, check website for additional short-term fellowships
Objective: To support sustained research in topics relating to book production and distribution in Britain during the hand-press period as well as studies of authorship, reading and collecting based on the examination of British books published in that period
Subject: Bibliographic history, history of the book trades, publishing history

80 Paul Mellon Centre Rome Fellowship

Awarding body: The Paul Mellon Centre for Studies in British Art
Address: Paul Mellon Centre for Studies in British Art, 16 Bedford Sq, London WC1B 3JA
Tel: 020 7580 0311
Fax: 020 7636 6730
Email: grants@paul-mellon-centre. ac.uk
Web: www.paul-mellon-centre.ac.uk
Contact: Fellowships and Grants Manager
Award: One 3-month fellowship awarded annually, full residential accommodation at the British School in Rome, £2,300 honorarium plus £7,500 towards replacement teaching cost for UK university staff, £6,000 stipend for independent scholars, applicants must be competent in spoken and written Italian, closing date 15 Jan
Objective: To support research of Grand Tour subjects in relation to Anglo-Italian artistic or cultural relations
Subject: Grand Tour subjects, Anglo-Italian artistic and visual cultural relations

81   Radcliffe Institute Fellowships

Awarding body: Radcliffe Institute for Advanced Study – Harvard University (USA)
Address: Radcliffe Institute for Advanced Study, 8 Garden St, Byerly Hall, Cambridge, MA 02138, USA
Tel: (001) 617 496 1324
Fax: (001) 617 495 8136
Email: fellowships@radcliffe.harvard.edu
Web: www.radcliffe.harvard.edu
Contact: Application Office
Award: Value up to US$70,000 for 1 year, plus funds for projects and relocation where relevant, residence in Boston required, open to those with at least 2 years' postdoctoral experience, closing date 1 Oct
Objective: To support scholars of exceptional promise and demonstrable accomplishment who wish to pursue work in academic and professional fields and in the creative arts
Subject: Any subject

82   Research Grants for Getty Scholars and Visiting Scholars; Pre- and Postdoctoral Fellowships

Awarding body: Getty Foundation (USA)
Address: Getty Foundation, 1200 Getty Center Dr, Suite 800, Los Angeles, CA 90049-1685, USA
Tel: (001) 310 440 7374
Fax: (001) 310 440 7703
Email: researchgrants@getty.edu
Web: www.getty.edu/foundation/funding/residential/
Contact: Getty Residential Scholar and Visiting Scholar Grants
Award: Salary replacement (value max US$65,000) and housing for Getty scholars for 3–9 months, closing date 1 Nov
Objective: To enable emerging scholars to complete their dissertations or to expand them for publication, or to enable established scholars, artists or writers to pursue their own projects free of academic obligation, while in residence at the Getty Research Institute
Subject: Humanities and the history of art

83   Residencies at the Rockefeller Foundation Bellagio Center

Awarding body: Rockefeller Foundation (USA)
Address: Institute of International Education (IIE), Bellagio Competition, 809 United Nations Plaza, 7th Floor, New York, NY 10017, USA
Tel: (001) 212 984 5537
Email: bellagio_res@iie.org
Web: www.rockefellerfoundation.org/bellagio-center/residency-program
Contact: Surabhi Lal, Program Officer
Award: One-month residencies, including room and board for the scholar and their partner/spouse, closing date 1 Dec
Objective: To bring together people of diverse expertise and backgrounds in a thought-provoking and collaborative environment; to promote innovation and impact on a wide range of global issues, allows for disciplined work and collaboration, uninterrupted by the usual professional and personal demands
Subject: Any subject, particularly within areas of basic survival strategies, global health, climate and environment, urbanisation and social and economic security

84 Robert H Smith International Center for Jefferson Studies Short-Term Fellowships

Awarding body: Robert H Smith International Center for Jefferson Studies (USA)
Address: Fellowship Committee, Robert H Smith International Center for Jefferson Studies, Monticello, PO Box 316, Charlottesville, Virginia 22902, USA
Tel: (001) 434 984 7500
Fax: (001) 434 296 1992
Email: ICJSfellowships@monticello.org
Web: www.monticello.org/research/fellowships/shortterm.html
Award: Short-term fellowships for 1–4 months for doctoral students and postdoctoral scholars, US$2,000 per month plus travel costs for scholars from the US and Canada, US$3,000 per month plus travel costs for international scholars
Objective: To allow scholars access to Monticello's expert staff and research holdings at the Jefferson Library as well as those of the University of Virginia
Subject: Jefferson-related projects, at least one fellowship will be reserved for related research topics in African-American history and in archaeology

85 Robert M Kingdon Fellowship in Judeo-Christian Religious Studies

Awarding body: Institute for Research in the Humanities (USA)
Address: Institute for Research in the Humanities, University of Wisconsin-Madison, 432 East Campus Mall, Room 221, Madison, WI 53706, USA
Tel: (001) 608 262 3855
Fax: (001) 608 265 4173
Email: awharris2@wisc.edu
Web: http://irh.wisc.edu/
Contact: Ann Harris, Administrative Assistant
Award: 1–2 available, stipend $50,000, access to the university libraries, the Institute's support services, and office space at the Institute, closing date 15 Nov
Objective: For residence at the Institute
Subject: Historical, literary and philosophical studies of the Judaeo-Christian religious tradition and its role in society from antiquity to the present

86 Robert Schuman Scholarships

Awarding body: European Parliament
Address: European Parliament, Europe House, 32 Smith Square, London SW1P 3EU
Tel: (00352) 4300 248 82
Email: stages@europarl.europa.eu
Web: www.europarl.europa.eu
Contact: European Parliament Traineeship Office
Award: Tenable for 5 months at the Secretariat of the European Parliament, closing dates 15 Oct, 15 May
Objective: To promote understanding of the European Parliament's role
Subject: European Parliament or the European Union organisation

87 Rome Scholarships and Fellowships in Ancient, Medieval and Later Italian Studies

Awarding body: British School at Rome (BSR)
Address: BSR, British Academy, 10 Carlton House Terrace, London SW1Y 5AH
Tel: 020 7969 5202
Fax: 020 7969 5401
Email: bsr@britac.ac.uk
Web: www.bsr.ac.uk
Contact: BSR London Office
Award: Nine-month residency, value £444 (scholarship) or £475 (fellowship) per month, plus board and lodging, for postgraduate and early postdoctoral research, closing date mid Jan
Objective: To allow scholars engaged in research to spend a period of time in Rome
Subject: Archaeology, art history, history, society and culture of Italy

88 Sainsbury Research Unit for the Arts of Africa, Oceania and the Americas Visiting Fellowships

Awarding body: University of East Anglia
Address: Sainsbury Research Unit for the Arts of Africa, Oceania and the Americas, University of East Anglia, Norwich Research Park,Norwich NR4 7TJ
Tel: 01603 592498
Fax: 01603 259401
Email: admin.sru@uea.ac.uk
Web: www.sru.uea.ac.uk
Contact: Admissions Secretary
Award: Two stipendiary residential fellowships offered annually, for postdoctoral research, open to scholars from the UK or overseas, tenable for 2–3 months
Objective: To support research for publication
Subject: Ethnohistory, art history, anthropology, archaeology, arts of Africa, Oceania and the Americas

89 Schomburg Center Scholars in Residence

Awarding body: Schomburg Center for Research in Black Culture (USA)
Address: Scholars-in-Residence Program, Schomburg Center for Research in Black Culture, 515 Malcolm X Blvd, New York, NY 10037-1801, USA
Tel: (001) 212 491 2228
Email: sir@nypl.org
Web: www.nypl.org/help/about-nypl/ fellowships-institutes/schomburg-center-scholars-in-residency/
Award: Value US$30,000 for 6 months, open to foreign nationals with 3 years' residence in the US immediately preceding the application deeadline, closing date 1 Nov
Objective: To encourage research and writing on the history, literature and cultures of the peoples of Africa and the African diaspora, to promote interaction among the participants, and to support dissemination of the research
Subject: History, literature and culture of peoples of African descent

90 School of Historical Studies Membership

Awarding body: Institute for Advanced Study, School of Historical Studies (USA)
Address: School of Historical Studies, Institute for Advanced Study, Einstein Dr, Princeton, NJ 08540, USA
Email: mzelazny@ias.edu
Web: http://www.hs.ias.edu/application
Contact: Administrative Officer
Award: Approx 40 offered for a single term or a full academic year to candidates of any nationality with a PhD and substantial publications, residence in Princeton during term time is required, scholars may apply for a stipend or if they have other resources for a non-stipendiary membership, some short-term visitorships without stipend also available, closing date 1 Nov
Objective: To promote intellectual enquiry, research and writing
Subject: Open to all fields of historical research, especially history of Western, Near Eastern and Asian civilisations, with particular emphasis upon Greek and Roman civilisation, the history of Europe (medieval, early modern and modern), the Islamic world, East Asian studies, art history, the history of science and philosophy, modern international relations and music studies

91 Shelby Cullom Davis Center for Historical Studies Research Fellowships

Awarding body: Shelby Cullom Davis Center for Historical Studies (USA)
Address: Shelby Cullom Davis Center for Historical Studies, Princeton University, 129 Dickinson Hall, Princeton, NJ 08544-1017, USA

Tel: (001) 609 258 4997
Fax: (001) 609 258 5326
Email: davisctr@princeton.edu
Web: www.princeton.edu/dav/
Contact: Philip Nord, Director
Award: For 1 or 2 semesters, open to those holding the doctorate and typically holding positions at universities
Objective: To enable scholars in historical studies to pursue postdoctoral research projects at the Center and contribute actively to the seminar
Subject: Topic changes every two years, for 2014–16 it is 'In the aftermath of catastrophe'

92 Society for the Humanities Fellowships

Awarding body: Society for the Humanities (USA)
Address: Society for the Humanities, AD White House, 27 East Ave, Cornell University, Ithaca, NY 14853-1101, USA
Tel: (001) 607 255 9274
Email: humctr-mailbox@cornell.edu
Web: www.arts.cornell.edu/sochum/
Contact: Program Administrator
Award: 6–8 available, value US$45,000, for 1 year, to be spent mainly at Cornell University, plus US$2,000 travel expenses for applicants from outside North America, applicants must have received the PhD by 1 Jan of year of application, closing date 1 Oct
Objective: To promote interdisciplinary research in the humanities
Subject: Humanities, topics related to theme set by Society for the Humanities (2014–15 theme is 'Sensation')

93 Solmsen Postdoctoral Fellowships

Awarding body: Institute for Research in the Humanities (USA)
Address: Institute for Research in the Humanities, University of Wisconsin-Madison, 432 East Campus Mall, Room 221, Madison, WI 53706, USA
Tel: (001) 608 262 3855
Fax: (001) 608 265 4173
Email: awharris2@wisc.edu
Web: http://irh.wisc.edu/
Contact: Ann Harris, Administrative Assistant
Award: 4–5 available, stipend US$50,000, access to the university libraries, the Institute's support services, and office space at the Institute, closing date 15 Nov
Objective: For residence at the Institute
Subject: Classical to Renaissance up to 1700, with a European focus

94 Stanford Humanities Center External Faculty Fellowships

Awarding body: Stanford Humanities Center (USA)
Address: Stanford Humanities Center, 424 Santa Teresa St, Room 151, Stanford, CA 94305-4015, USA
Tel: (001) 650 723 3054
Fax: (001) 650 723 1895
Email: shc-fellowships@stanford.edu
Web: http://shc.stanford.edu/
Award: Up to 8 external faculty fellowships awarded for the academic year (Sept–June), value max US$70,000 with a housing/travel allowance max US$30,000, applicants should be at least 3 years beyond receipt of the PhD by the beginning of the fellowship term, closing date 1 Oct
Objective: The Center seeks both junior and senior applicants whose research is likely to contribute to intellectual exchange among a diverse group of scholars
Subject: Any subject

95 Thomas K McCraw Fellowship in US Business History

Awarding body: Harvard Business School (USA)
Address: Connell 301A, Rock Center 104, Harvard Business School, Soldiers Field, Boston, MA 02163, USA
Email: wfriedman@hbs.edu
Web: www.library.hbs.edu/hc/researchfellowships/index.html
Contact: Walter A Friedman
Award: One available annually, value US$7,000, open to established scholars worldwide who study American business or economic history, duration at least 2 months, closing date 15 Sept
Objective: To allow established scholars in business history to spend a period of time in residence at Harvard Business School
Subject: Business history, economic history

96   Wyndham Deedes
Memorial Travel Scholarship

Awarding body: Anglo-Israel
Association
Address: Wyndham Deedes Memorial
Trust Fund, PO Box 47819, London
NW11 7WD
Tel: 020 8458 1284
Fax: 020 8458 3484
Email: info@angloisraelassociation.
com
Web: www.angloisraelassociation.com
Contact: Mrs Ruth Saunders
Award: Grants of up to £2,000
towards expenses incurred in visiting
Israel, applicants must spend at
least 6 weeks in Israel and submit a
report of at least 5,000 words within
12 months of return from Israel,
application forms on website, closing
date 31 July
Objective: To enable graduates
of British universities to make an
intensive study of some aspect of life
in Israel in an area of direct interest to
those working in that field in the UK
Subject: Any

4   Library research grants

97   Abba P Schwartz Research Fellowship

Awarding body: John F Kennedy Library Foundation (USA)
Address: John F Kennedy Library, Columbia Point, Boston, MA 02125, USA
Tel: (001) 617 514 1631
Fax: (001) 617 514 1625
Email: kennedy.library@nara.gov
Web: www.jfklibrary.org
Contact: Grant and Fellowship Co-ordinator
Award: One awarded annually, value max US$3,100, closing date 15 Aug
Objective: To support research at the Library
Subject: Immigration, naturalisation or refugee policy

98   Ahmanson-Getty Postdoctoral Fellowships

Awarding body: UCLA Center for 17th- and 18th-Century Studies (USA)
Address: Center for 17th- and 18th-Century Studies, 310 Royce Hall, UCLA, Los Angeles, CA 90095-1404, USA
Tel: (001) 310 206 8552
Fax: (001) 310 206 8577
Email: c1718cs@humnet.ucla.edu
Web: www.c1718cs.ucla.edu
Contact: Fellowships Co-ordinator
Award: Up to 4 annually, value US$39,264 for the academic year, for those who received the PhD in the last 6 years, closing date 1 Feb
Objective: To encourage the participation of junior scholars in the William Andrews Clark Library and Center
Subject: Theme for 2014–15 is 'Explorations, encounters, and the circulation of knowledge, 1600–1830'

99   Alfred D Chandler Jr Travel Fellowship

Awarding body: Harvard Business School (USA)
Address: Connell 301A, Harvard Business School, Boston, MA 02163, USA
Email: wfriedman@hbs.edu
Web: www.hbs.edu/businesshistory/fellowships.html
Contact: Walter A Friedman
Award: Value US$1,000–US$3,000, open to graduate students or non-tenured faculty whose research requires travel to the Boston-Cambridge area, or to Harvard students who are required to travel away from Cambridge, MA, closing date 1 Nov
Objective: To facilitate library and archival research that seeks to relate historical reality to underlying economic theories of business development
Subject: Economic history, broadly defined

100   American Philosophical Society Library Resident Research Fellowships

Awarding body: American Philosophical Society (USA)
Address: Library Resident Research Fellowships, American Philosophical Society, 105 South 5th St, Philadelphia, PA 19106-3386, USA
Tel: (001) 215 440 3400
Email: libfellows@amphilsoc.org
Web: www.amphilsoc.org/grants/library/
Award: Value US$2,500 per month for up to 3 months, for PhD students and beyond, closing date 1 Mar
Objective: To enable research in the collections of the Society
Subject: Any subject covered in the Society's collections

101   American Society for 18th-Century Studies – Clark Fellowships

Awarding body: UCLA Center for 17th- and 18th-Century Studies (USA)
Address: Center for 17th- and 18th-Century Studies, 10745 Dickson Plaza, 310 Royce Hall, UCLA, Los Angeles, CA 90095-1404, USA
Tel: (001) 310 206 8552
Fax: (001) 310 206 8577
Email: c1718cs@humnet.ucla.edu
Web: www.c1718cs.ucla.edu
Contact: Fellowships Co-ordinator
Award: Value US$2,500, for 1 month, number offered varies, open to postdoctoral members of ASECS, closing date 1 Feb
Objective: For study at the William Andrews Clark Memorial Library
Subject: The Restoration or the 18th century

102   American Society for 18th-Century Studies Library Fellowships

Awarding body: American Society for 18th-Century Studies (ASECS) (USA)
Address: ASECS, PO Box 7867, Wake Forest University, Winston-Salem, NC 27109, USA
Tel: (001) 336 727 4694
Fax: (001) 336 727 4697
Email: asecs@wfu.edu
Web: http://asecs.press.jhu.edu/
Award: Offered to graduate or postdoctoral members of ASECS, for 1 month's support at one of 12 affliated research institutes, contact the relevant library in the first instance
Objective: To promote and sustain the study of the 18th century and support scholars' travel to collections
Subject: 18th-century studies

103   Arthur M Schlesinger Jr Fellowship

Awarding body: John F Kennedy Library Foundation (USA)
Address: John F Kennedy Library, Columbia Point, Boston, MA 02125, USA
Tel: (001) 617 514 1631
Fax: (001) 617 514 1625
Email: kennedy.library@nara.gov
Web: www.jfklibrary.org
Contact: Grant and Fellowships Co-ordinator
Award: Value up to US$5,000, closing date 15 Aug
Objective: To support research at the Library
Subject: Foreign policy of Kennedy years, especially with regard to the western hemisphere, or Kennedy domestic policy, especially with regard to racial justice and to the conservation of natural resources

104 Audrey and William H Helfand Fellowship in the History of Medicine and Public Health

Awarding body: New York Academy of Medicine (USA)
Address: Historical Collections, New York Academy of Medicine, 1216 5th Ave, New York, NY 10029, USA
Tel: (001) 212 822 7313
Fax: (001) 212 423 0273
Email: history@nyam.org
Web: www.nyam.org/grants/helfand. html
Contact: Arlene Shaner
Award: Stipend of up to US$5,000 to support travel, lodging and incidental expenses for a flexible period of approximately 1 month for a scholar in residence at the Academy library
Objective: To support research using the Academy Library's resources for scholarly study of the history of medicine or public health, with a preference for those using visual materials
Subject: History of medicine or public health

105 Beckman Center for the History of Chemistry Travel Grants

Awarding body: Chemical Heritage Foundation (CHF) (USA)
Address: CHF, 315 Chestnut St, Philadelphia, PA 19106-2702, USA
Tel: (001) 215 925 2222
Fax: (001) 215 925 6195
Email: travelgrants@chemheritage. org
Web: www.chemheritage.org/ research/fellowships-and-travel-grants/beckman-center-fellowships/ travel-grants.aspx
Contact: Fellowship Co-ordinator
Award: To cover travel and lodging expenses for researchers to use the CHF's Othmer Library and historical archives and collections, in the region of US$750 per week for 1–4 weeks, no deadline
Objective: To support the use of the CHF's Othmer Library and historical archives and collections
Subject: History of science, history of chemistry and the chemical process

106 Beinecke Library Visiting Fellowships

Awarding body: Beinecke Rare Book and Manuscript Library (USA)
Address: Beinecke Rare Book and Manuscript Library, Yale University, PO Box 208240, New Haven, CT 06520-8240, USA
Email: beinecke.fellowships@yale.edu
Web: http://beinecke.library.yale.edu/ programs-events/fellowship-program/
Contact: Director
Award: For 1 month between Sept and May, value US$4,000 living allowance, plus round-trip travel to New Haven, deadline 7 Dec
Objective: To support postdoctoral or equivalent research in the Beinecke collections
Subject: Medieval, Renaissance and 18th-century studies, art history, photography, American studies, history of printing, music and modernism in art and literature, literary papers and early manuscripts and rare books in literature, theology and history

107 Caird North American Fellowship

Awarding body: National Maritime Museum/John Carter Brown Library (USA)
Address: National Maritime Museum, Greenwich, London SE10 9NF
Tel: 020 8312 6716
Fax: 020 8312 6521
Email: research@rmg.ac.uk
Web: www.nmm.ac.uk
Contact: Research Executive
Award: Value £5,000 towards 3 months' living and research expenses in the US and airfare, open to those who have completed or are near completion of the PhD, closing date 25 Oct
Objective: To support advanced research in collections in the USA, based at the John Carter Brown Library in Providence, RI, but with the opportunity to travel along the east coast
Subject: Maritime history of the US and Britain

108 Caird Senior Research Fellowship

Awarding body: National Maritime Museum/Royal Observatory Greenwich
Address: National Maritime Museum, Greenwich, London SE10 9NF
Tel: 020 8312 6716
Fax: 020 8312 6592
Email: research@rmg.ac.uk
Web: www.nmm.ac.uk/researchers/fellowships-and-internships/
Contact: Research Executive
Award: Value £20,000 pa for 1 year, postdoctoral, closing date 28 Oct
Objective: To support research utilising the Museum's collections
Subject: Maritime history, 17th–19th centuries

109 Caird Short-Term Research Fellowships

Awarding body: National Maritime Museum/Royal Observatory Greenwich
Address: National Maritime Museum, Greenwich, London SE10 9NF
Tel: 020 8312 6716
Fax: 020 8312 6592
Email: research@rmg.ac.uk
Web: www.rmg.ac.uk
Contact: Research Executive
Award: Value £1,600 per month for up to 3 months, open to scholars from abroad or a distance from London, closing date 25 Oct
Objective: To support research utilising the Museum's collections
Subject: Maritime history, 17th–19th centuries

110 Center for History of Science Scholarships

Awarding body: Center for History of Science (Centrum för Vetenskapshistoria) – Royal Swedish Academy of Sciences (Sweden)
Address: Center for History of Science, Box 50005, SE-104 05 Stockholm, Sweden
Tel: (0046) 8673 9500
Fax: (0046) 8673 9598
Email: centrum@kva.se
Web: www.center.kva.se
Contact: Professor Karl Grandin, Director
Award: Two awarded, value SEK25,000, applications should be sent at least 1 year in advance
Objective: To allow non-Swedish researchers to use the archives at the Center
Subject: History of science

111 Clark Short-Term Fellowships

Awarding body: UCLA Center for 17th- and 18th-Century Studies (USA)
Address: Center for 17th- and 18th-Century Studies, 310 Royce Hall, UCLA, Los Angeles, CA 90095-1404, USA
Tel: (001) 310 206 8552
Fax: (001) 310 206 8577
Email: c1718cs@humnet.ucla.edu
Web: www.c1718cs.ucla.edu
Contact: Fellowships Coordinator
Award: Value US$2,500 per month, 1–3 months in residence, for holders of the PhD or equivalent, closing date 1 Feb
Objective: For study at the William Andrews Clark Memorial Library
Subject: 17th- and 18th-century studies

112 Cullman Center Fellowships

Awarding body: Dorothy and Lewis B Cullman Center for Scholars and Writers – New York Public Library (USA)
Address: Stephen A Schwarzman Building, 5th Ave and 42nd St, Room 225, New York, NY 10018-2788, USA
Tel: (001) 212 930 0084
Fax: (001) 212 930 0040
Email: csw@nypl.org
Web: www.nypl.org/locations/ schwarzman/cullman-center-scholars-writers/
Contact: Fellowships Administrator, New York Public Library
Award: Up to 15 fellowships pa for scholars who need to work in the Stephen A Schwarzman Building of the New York Public Library, value up to US$65,000 plus office facilities and full access to the Library's physical and electronic resources, funding not

available for research leading directly to a degree, closing date 30 Sept
Objective: To promote dynamic communication about literature and scholarship at the very highest level
Subject: Anthropology, art, geography, history, languages and literature, philosophy, politics, popular culture, psychology, religion, sociology and sport

113 Dana and David Dornsife Fellowship

Awarding body: Huntington Library, Art Collections and Botanical Gardens (USA)
Address: Committee on Fellowships, The Huntington, 1151 Oxford Rd, San Marino, CA 91108, USA
Tel: (001) 626 405 2194
Email: cpowell@huntington.org
Web: www.huntington.org
Contact: Chair
Award: Value US$50,000, for 9–12 months, postdoctoral, closing date 15 Nov
Objective: To support research in a field relevant to the Huntington's collections
Subject: British and American literature, history, art history and history of science and medicine

114 Dianne Woest Fellowship in the Arts and Humanities

Awarding body: Historic New Orleans Collection (USA)
Address: Historic New Orleans Collection, 533 Royal St, New Orleans, LA 70130, USA
Tel: (001) 504 598 7171
Email: asonw@hnoc.org
Web: www.hnoc.org
Contact: Mr Jason Wiese, Assistant Director, Williams Research Center
Award: Value US$4,000 per month for 1–3 months, open to doctoral candidates, academic and museum professionals and independent scholars fluent in English, US citizenship not required, closing date 1 Nov
Objective: To promote and support scholarly research in the history and culture of Louisiana and the Gulf South
Subject: Arts and humanities particular to Louisiana and the Gulf South

115 Eccles Centre Visiting Professorships, Fellowships and Postgraduate Awards

Awarding body: British Association for American Studies (BAAS)
Address: BAAS, School of Humanities, Chancellor's Building, Keele University, Keele, Staffs ST5 5BG
Email: awards@baas.ac.uk
Web: www.baas.ac.uk
Contact: Professor Ian Bell (i.f.a.bell@ams.keele.ac.uk)
Award: Various awards, available to graduate students and postdoctoral scholars from outside London, amount and duration vary depending on applicant's location, closing date 31 Jan

Objective: To support scholars who need to visit London to use the British Library's collections relating to North America
Subject: American studies

116 Ernest Hemingway Research Grants

Awarding body: John F Kennedy Library Foundation (USA)
Address: John F Kennedy Library, Columbia Point, Boston, MA 02125, USA
Tel: (001) 617 514 1624
Fax: (001) 617 514 1625
Email: kennedy.library@nara.gov
Web: www.jfklibrary.org
Contact: Grant and Fellowships Co-ordinator
Award: For living, travel and related costs, value US$200–US$1,000, closing date 1 Nov
Objective: To enable use of the Ernest Hemingway Collection
Subject: Hemingway and related studies

117 Friends of Princeton University Library Research Grants

Awarding body: Princeton University Library (USA)
Address: Library Research Grant Committee, 1 Washington Rd, Princeton, NJ 08544, USA
Tel: (001) 609 285 3155
Fax: (001) 609 285 2324
Email: pulgrant@princeton.edu
Web: www.princeton.edu/rbsc/fellowships/f_ships.html
Contact: Library Research Grant Committee
Award: Value up to US$3,500 to defray travel and living expenses during tenure of the grant (normally 1 month), closing date 15 Jan

Objective: To allow consultation and study at the Princeton University Library
Subject: Any subject, though the proposal should address specifically the relevance to the proposed research of unique resources found in the Princeton University Library collections

118   Gerald R Ford Foundation Research Travel Grants Program

Awarding body: Gerald R Ford Foundation (USA)
Address: Gerald R Ford Library, 1000 Beal Ave, Ann Arbor, MI 48109, USA
Tel: (001) 734 205 0557
Fax: (001) 734 205 0571
Email: ford.library@nara.gov
Web: http://www.fordlibrarymuseum. gov/library/foundationgrants.asp
Contact: Jeremy Schmidt, Grants Coordinator / Archivist
Award: Value up to US$2,000 to defray living, travel and related expenses incurred while conducting research at the Library, closing dates 15 Mar, 15 Sept
Objective: To support research at the Gerald R Ford Presidential Library
Subject: US government, domestic and foreign issues, policies and political affairs in the 1970s

119   Getty Library Research Grants

Awarding body: Getty Foundation (USA)
Address: Getty Foundation, 1200 Getty Center Dr, Suite 800, Los Angeles, CA 90049-1685, USA
Tel: (001) 310 440 7390
Fax: (001) 310 440 7703
Email: researchgrants@getty.edu
Web: www.getty.edu/foundation/ funding/residential/

Contact: Library Research Grants
Award: Offered annually, value US$500–US$2,500 for up to 3 months, closing date 15 Oct
Objective: To provide support for costs relating to travel and living expenses to scholars whose projects would benefit from use of the Library's special collections
Subject: History of art

120   Gladstone's Library Scholarships

Awarding body: Gladstone's Library
Address: Gladstone's Library, St Deiniol's, Church Lane, Hawarden, Flintshire CH5 3DF
Tel: 01244 532350
Fax: 01244 520643
Email: peter.francis@gladlib.org
Web: www.st-deiniols.com/courses/ scholarships/
Contact: The Warden, Peter Francis
Award: Various scholarships available covering use of the library, dinner, bed and breakfast for any period from a week to several months, closing date 1 Nov
Objective: To enable scholars to use the library collections
Subject: Theology and Victorian studies

121 Grants-in-Aid for Research at the Rockefeller Archive Center

Awarding body: Rockefeller Archive Center (USA)
Address: Rockefeller Archive Center, 15 Dayton Ave, Sleepy Hollow, NY 10591, USA
Tel: (001) 914 631 4505
Fax: (001) 914 631 6017
Email: archive@rockarch.org
Web: http://www.rockarch.org/Grants/generalgia.php
Contact: Grant Program Administrator
Award: Grants of up to US$4,000 for expenses related to research conducted at the Center, closing date 1 Nov
Objective: To foster, promote and support research by serious scholars in the collections located at the Center
Subject: History of philanthropy

122 Hagley Exploratory Research Grants

Awarding body: Hagley Museum and Library (USA)
Address: Center for the History of Business, Technology, and Society, PO Box 3630, Wilmington, DE 19807-0630, USA
Tel: (001) 302 658 2400
Web: http://www.hagley.org/library-exploratorygrant
Contact: Carol Ressler Lockman
Award: Stipend of US$400, low-cost accommodation available on a first-come, first-served basis, to support a 1-week visit preliminary to application for Henry Belin du Pont Research Grant, closing dates 31 Oct, 31 Mar, 30 Jun
Objective: To support exploratory research in the Hagley Museum and Library and to help scholars identify pertinent items in the collections

Subject: History of business, technology and science, and the library, archival and artefact collections of the Hagley Museum and Library

123 Harry S Truman Library Research Grants

Awarding body: Harry S Truman Library Institute (USA)
Address: Harry S Truman Library Institute, 500 W US Hwy 24, Independence, MO 64050, USA
Tel: (001) 816 833 8248
Fax: (001) 816 833 8299
Email: sullivan.hstli@gmail.com
Web: www.trumanlibrary.org/grants/
Contact: Lisa Sullivan, Grants Administrator
Award: Number varies, offered biannually, value US$2,500, for 1–3 weeks at the Library, primarily graduate and postdoctoral, closing dates 1 Oct, 1 Apr
Objective: To enable graduate students and postdoctoral scholars to visit the Library, preference may be given to projects that have an application to enduring public or foreign policy and have a high probability of publication
Subject: Research on some aspect of the life and career of Harry S Truman and the Truman administration

124   Henry Belin du Pont Dissertation Fellowships

Awarding body: Hagley Museum and Library (USA)
Address: Center for the History of Business, Technology, and Society, PO Box 3630, Wilmington, DE 19807-0630, USA
Tel: (001) 302 658 2400
Email: clockman@hagley.org
Web: www.hagley.org/library-fellowships/
Contact: Carol Ressler Lockman
Award: Residential for 4 months, value US$6,500, accommodation may be available on the Museum grounds, closing date 15 Nov
Objective: To enable scholars to pursue advanced research and study in the library, archival and artefact collections of the Hagley Museum and Library. Scholars are expected to participate fully in seminars and programmes during tenure
Subject: History of American enterprise

125   Houghton Library Visiting Fellowships

Awarding body: Houghton Library – Harvard University (USA)
Address: Houghton Library, Harvard University, Cambridge, MA 02138, USA
Tel: (001) 617 495 2441
Email: duhaime@fas.harvard.edu
Web: http://hcl.harvard.edu/houghton/
Contact: Fellowship Selection Committee
Award: Eight short-term fellowships available, value up to US$3,000, residence at Harvard University is expected for at least 1 month, closing date 17 Jan
Objective: To assist scholars who must travel to work with the Library's collections

Subject: Subjects incorporated in the Library's holdings, including American literary manuscripts, philosophy, religion, history of science, music, printing and graphic arts, dance and theatre

126   J B Harley Research Fellowships in the History of Cartography

Awarding body: J B Harley Fellowships
Address: J B Harley Fellowships, Map Archivist, Advice and Records Knowledge Department, The National Archives, Kew, Surrey TW9 4DU
Tel: 020 8392 5330 ext 2492
Email: rose.mitchell@nationalarchives.gsi.gov.uk
Web: www.maphistory.info/harley.html
Contact: Rose Mitchell, Hon Secretary
Award: 2–4 grants annually, value £400 per week for 2–4 weeks, closing date 1 Nov
Objective: For doctoral, postdoctoral or equivalent research, to promote the historical cartographical material available in London and other parts of the UK
Subject: History of cartography

127   J Franklin Jameson Fellowship in American History

Awarding body: American Historical Association (AHA) (USA)
Address: J Franklin Jameson Fellowship, AHA, 400 A St, SE Washington, DC 20003, USA
Tel: (001) 202 544 2422
Fax: (001) 202 544 8307
Email: aha@historians.org
Web: www.historians.org/prizes/ Grants.cfm
Contact: Administrative Office Assistant
Award: Awarded biennially, value US$5,000 for 2–3 months at the Library of Congress, postdoctoral, with the PhD being received within the last 7 years, closing date 15 March
Objective: To support significant scholarly research in the collections of the Library of Congress
Subject: American history

128   Kanner Fellowship in British Studies

Awarding body: UCLA Center for 17th- and 18th-Century Studies (USA)
Address: Center for 17th- and 18th-Century Studies, 310 Royce Hall, UCLA, Los Angeles, CA 90095-1404, USA
Tel: (001) 310 206 8552
Fax: (001) 310 206 8577
Email: c1718cs@humnet.ucla.edu
Web: www.c1718cs.ucla.edu
Contact: Fellowships Co-ordinator
Award: Value US$7,500, for 3 months, pre- and postdoctoral, closing date 1 Feb
Objective: For study at the William Andrews Clark Memorial Library
Subject: British history and culture

129   Katherine F Pantzer Jr Fellowship in Descriptive Bibliography

Awarding body: Houghton Library – Harvard University (USA)
Address: Houghton Library, Harvard University, Cambridge, MA 02138, USA
Tel: (001) 617 495 2441
Email: duhaime@fas.harvard.edu
Web: http://hcl.harvard.edu/libraries/ houghton/public_programs/visiting_ fellowships.cfm#overview
Contact: Fellowship Selection Committee
Award: Stipend of up to US$3,000 per month for up to 12 months (US$36,000), fellows expected to be in residence at Houghton Library for the duration of the fellowship, closing date 17 Jan
Objective: To assist scholarly research in descriptive bibliography at Houghton Library
Subject: Subjects incorporated in the Library's holdings, including American literary manuscripts, philosophy, religion, history of science, music, printing and graphic arts, dance and theatre

130 Kennedy Research Grants

Awarding body: John F Kennedy Library Foundation (USA)
Address: John F Kennedy Library, Columbia Point, Boston, MA 02125, USA
Tel: (001) 617 514 1629
Fax: (001) 617 514 1625
Email: kennedy.library@nara.gov
Web: www.jfklibrary.org
Contact: Grant and Fellowship Co-ordinator
Award: Value US$500–US$2,500, preference given to PhD dissertation-related research, or revision for publication, using newly opened or relatively unused areas of the Library's holdings, closing dates 15 Mar, 15 Aug
Objective: To enable residence, travel and related costs while working at the Library
Subject: Any subject relating to the Library's holdings, American history

131 Marjorie Kovler Fellowship

Awarding body: John F Kennedy Library Foundation (USA)
Address: John F Kennedy Library, Columbia Point, Boston, MA 02125, USA
Tel: (001) 617 514 1629
Email: kennedy.library@nara.gov
Web: www.jfklibrary.org/
JFK+Library+and+Museum/
Kennedy+Library+Foundation/
Programs+and+Library+Support/
(click on Research Grants and Fellowships)
Contact: Grant and Fellowships Co-ordinator
Award: Awarded annually, value max US$2,500, closing date 15 Aug

Objective: To support travel to the Kennedy Library for a scholar in the production of a substantial work in the area of foreign intelligence and the presidency or a related topic
Subject: Foreign intelligence and the presidency

132 Mellon Postdoctoral Fellowship

Awarding body: Huntington Library, Art Collections and Botanical Gardens (USA)
Address: Committee on Fellowships, The Huntington, 1151 Oxford Rd, San Marino, CA 91108, USA
Tel: (001) 626 405 2194
Email: cpowell@huntington.org
Web: www.huntington.org
Contact: Chair
Award: Value US$50,000, for 9–12 months, postdoctoral, closing date 15 Nov
Objective: To support research in a field relevant to the Huntington's collections
Subject: British and American literature, history, art history and history of science and medicine

133   Newberry Library Short-Term Fellowships

Awarding body: Newberry Library (USA)
Address: Newberry Library, 60 W Walton St, Chicago, IL 60610-7324, USA
Tel: (001) 312 255 3666
Email: research@newberry.org
Web: www.newberry.org/fellowships/
Contact: Office of Research and Academic Programs
Award: Various fellowships available, from 1–2 months, most stipends US$2,000 per month, open to postdoctoral scholars or PhD candidates, closing date 15 Jan
Objective: To support research that requires access to specific items in the Library's collections
Subject: Humanities

134   Paul Klemperer Fellowship in the History of Medicine

Awarding body: New York Academy of Medicine (USA)
Address: Historical Collections, New York Academy of Medicine, 1216 5th Ave, New York, NY 10029, USA
Tel: (001) 212 822 7313
Fax: (001) 212 423 0273
Email: history@nyam.org
Web: www.nyam.org/grants/klemperer.html
Contact: Arlene Shaner
Award: Stipend of up to US$5,000 to support travel, lodging and incidental expenses for a flexible period of approximately 1 month for a scholar in residence at the Academy library
Objective: To support research using the Academy Library's resources for scholarly study of the history of medicine
Subject: History of medicine

135   Roosevelt Institute Grants-in-Aid

Awarding body: Roosevelt Institute (USA)
Address: Grants Committee, Franklin and Eleanor Roosevelt Institute, 4079 Albany Post Rd, Hyde Park, NY 12538, USA
Web: http://rooseveltinstitute.org/projects/roosevelt-awards-research-grants/
Contact: Chairman, Grants Committee
Award: Grants of up to US$2,500, for research on the 'Roosevelt years' or clearly related subjects, to defray living, travel and related expenses incurred while conducting research at the Roosevelt Library, closing date 15 Nov
Objective: Designed to encourage younger scholars to expand on their knowledge and understanding of the Roosevelt period and to give support for research to Roosevelt scholars from the emerging democracies and the Third World
Subject: America in the Roosevelt period

136   Sackler Short-Term Research Fellowships

Awarding body: National Maritime Museum/Royal Observatory Greenwich
Address: National Maritime Museum, Greenwich, London SE10 9NF
Tel: 020 8312 6716
Fax: 020 8312 6592
Email: research@nmm.ac.uk
Web: www.rmg.co.uk/researchers/fellowships-and-internships/sackler-short-term-research-fellowship/
Contact: Research Executive
Award: Value £1,600 per month for up to 3 months, open to scholars from abroad or a distance from London, closing date 28 Oct
Objective: To support research utilising the Museum's collections, including the Royal Observatory
Subject: History of astronomy and navigational technology

137   Sackler-Caird Fellowship

Awarding body: National Maritime Museum/Royal Observatory Greenwich
Address: National Maritime Museum, Greenwich, London SE10 9NF
Tel: 020 8312 6716
Fax: 020 8312 6592
Email: research@rmg.co.uk
Web: www.nmm.ac.uk/researchers/fellowships-and-internships/
Contact: Research Department Executive
Award: Value £30,000 pa for up to 2 years, open to established researchers already in post at an academic institution, closing date 28 Oct
Objective: To support a sustained period of research utilising the Museum's collections
Subject: Maritime history, 17th–19th centuries

138   Schlesinger Library on the History of Women in America Dissertation Grants

Awarding body: Schlesinger Library (USA)
Address: Schlesinger Library, Radcliffe Institute for Advanced Study, Harvard University, 3 James St, Cambridge, MA 02138, USA
Tel: (001) 617 495 8647
Email: slgrants@radcliffe.edu
Web: www.radcliffe.harvard.edu/schlesinger-library/grants/dissertation-grants/
Contact: Grants Administrator
Award: Two available, value up to US$3,000, for doctoral dissertation students, non-US applicants should contact the Library before applying, closing date 25 Mar
Objective: To promote and support the use of the Schlesinger Library, priority will be given to those students whose projects require the use of materials found only in the Library's holdings
Subject: Subjects relating to the Library's holdings

139   Schlesinger Library on the History of Women Research Support Grants

Awarding body: Schlesinger Library (USA)
Address: Schlesinger Library, Radcliffe Institute for Advanced Study, Harvard University, 3 James St, Cambridge, MA 02138, USA
Tel: (001) 617 594 8647
Email: slgrants@radcliffe.edu
Web: www.radcliffe.harvard.edu/schlesinger-library/grants/research-support-grants/
Contact: Grants Administrator
Award: Value up to US$3,000, open to scholars whose projects require access to the holdings of the Library, non-US applicants should contact the Library before applying, closing date 16 Mar
Objective: To promote and support the use of the Schlesinger Library and Radcliffe Institute
Subject: Subjects relating to the Library's holdings

140   Theodora Bosanquet Bursaries

Awarding body: BFWG Charitable Foundation
Address: BFWG Charitable Foundation, 28 Great James St, London WC1N 3ES
Tel: 01732 321139
Email: jean.c@blueyonder.co.uk
Web: www.ffwg.org.uk
Contact: Grants Administrator
Award: 1–2 offered annually, value up to £600, for up to 4 weeks at a London hall of residence for women postgraduate or postdoctoral students, closing date 31 Oct
Objective: To support women postgraduate students who are carrying out research in English literature or history requiring the use of libraries and archives in London
Subject: English literature and history

141   Winterthur Dissertation Fellowships

Awarding body: Winterthur Museum, Garden and Library (USA)
Address: Academic Programs, 5105 Kennett Pike, Winterthur Museum, Garden and Library, Winterthur, DE 19735, USA
Tel: (001) 302 888 4637
Email: rkrill@winterthur.org
Web: www.winterthur.org/?p=535
Award: Offered annually to doctoral candidates, value of stipend US$7,000 per semester, for 1–2 semesters in residence, closing date 15 Jan
Objective: To enable doctoral candidates to conduct research for their dissertations
Subject: American art, decorative arts, material culture and history 1650–1930 (collections also include strong supporting British and Continental materials)

142   Winterthur Research Fellowships

Awarding body: Winterthur Museum, Garden and Library (USA)
Address: Academic Programs, 5105 Kennett Pike, Winterthur Museum, Garden and Library, Wilmington, DE 19735, USA
Tel: (001) 302 888 4637
Email: academicprograms@ winterthur.org
Web: www.winterthur.org/fellowship/
Award: Fifteen awarded annually, value US$1,750 per month, for 1–3 months in residence, open to doctoral students and academic staff, museum and independent scholars, closing date 15 Jan
Objective: For research
Subject: American art, decorative arts, material culture and history 1650–1930 (collections also include strong supporting British and Continental materials)

Objective: To foster the high-level use of the University of Wisconsin-Madison Library's holdings, and to make them better known and more accessible to a wider circle of scholars with PhDs or who are able to demonstrate a record of solid intellectual accomplishment
Subject: Humanities

143   University of Wisconsin-Madison Grants-in-Aid

Awarding body: Friends of the UW-Madison Libraries (USA)
Address: Friends of the UW-Madison Library, University of Wisconsin-Madison, 728 State St, Madison, WI 53706, USA
Tel: (001) 608 265 2505
Fax: (001) 608 265 2754
Email: friends@library.wisc.edu
Web: www.library.wisc.edu/friends/
Award: Several awarded annually of 1 month in duration, value US$2,000 each for North American recipients and US$3,000 for recipients elsewhere in the world, preference given to younger scholars, closing date 1 Feb

5   Miscellaneous awards

144   Aurelius Charitable Trust Grants

Awarding body: Aurelius Charitable Trust
Address: Aurelius Charitable Trust, Briarsmead, Old Rd, Buckland, Betchworth, Surrey RH3 7DU
Tel: 01737 842186
Email: philip.haynes@tiscali.co.uk
Contact: P E Haynes
Award: Value usually £500–£5,000, grants are only made to charitable bodies not individuals, trustees meet twice annually in Jan and July, please enclose SAE if corresponding by post
Objective: Intended as seed-corn funding to attract other funding or completion funding, not intended to cover administrative or general running costs
Subject: Conservation of culture inherited from the past, humanities

145   BSHS Special Projects Grants

Awarding body: British Society for the History of Science (BSHS)
Address: BSHS Executive Secretary, PO Box 3401, Norwich NR7 7JF
Email: office@bshs.org.uk
Web: www.bshs.org.uk/grants/special-projects-grants/
Contact: Executive Secretary
Award: Grants of £50–£1,500 for special projects, closing dates 31 Mar, 30 Sept
Objective: To support projects which will promote the general aims of the Society, not intended for straightforward academic research projects, which are covered under the Research Grants scheme
Subject: History of science, technology or medicine

146   Daiwa Foundation Awards

Awarding body: Daiwa Anglo-Japanese Foundation
Address: Daiwa Anglo-Japanese Foundation, Japan House, 13/14 Cornwall Terrace, London NW1 4QP
Tel: 020 7486 4348
Fax: 020 7486 2914
Email: grants@dajf.org.uk
Web: www.dajf.org.uk/grants-awards-prizes/overview/
Award: £7,000–£15,000 available for collaborative projects that enable British and Japanese partners to work together, preferably within the context of an institutional relationship, closing dates 31 Mar, 30 Sept
Objective: To support collaboration between UK and Japan partnerships with tangible long-term objectives
Subject: Projects that promote and enhance UK-Japan collaboration and understanding

147 Daiwa Foundation Small Grants

Awarding body: Daiwa Anglo-Japanese Foundation
Address: Daiwa Anglo-Japanese Foundation, Japan House, 13/14 Cornwall Terrace, London NW1 4QP
Tel: 020 7486 4348
Fax: 020 7486 2914
Email: grants@dajf.org.uk
Web: www.dajf.org.uk/grants-awards-prizes/overview/
Award: £3,000–£7,000 available to individuals, societies or other bodies in the UK or Japan to promote and support interaction between the two countries, closing dates 31 Mar, 30 Sept
Objective: To enable British and Japanese individuals and institutions to work together on collaborative projects and to encourage new initiatives
Subject: Projects that promote and enhance UK-Japan collaboration and understanding

148 Economic History Society Facility Grants for Undergraduate Students

Awarding body: Economic History Society
Address: Economic History Society, Department of Economic and Social History, University of Glasgow, Lilybank House, Bute Gardens, Glasgow G12 8RT
Tel: 0141 330 4662
Fax: 0141 330 4889
Email: ehsocsec@arts.gla.ac.uk
Web: www.ehs.org.uk
Contact: Administrative Secretary
Award: Value not normally over £250, applications to be made by students through supervisors/tutors, no closing date, not for purchase of books or materials or for conference attendance
Objective: To assist undergraduate students with expenses incurred in the preparation of economic and social history projects for final degree examinations
Subject: Economic and social history

149 Economic History Society Internships at the Ashmolean Museum, Oxford

Awarding body: Economic History Society
Address: Economic History Society, Department of Economic and Social History, University of Glasgow, Lilybank House, Bute Gardens, Glasgow G12 8RT
Tel: 0141 330 4662
Fax: 0141 330 4889
Email: nick.mayhew@ashmus.ox.ac.uk
Web: www.ehs.org.uk
Contact: Nick Mayhew
Award: Value £1,000 per month for 3 months, open to postgraduate students and early-career researchers in economic history, possible research topics detailed on website, closing date 1 May
Objective: To give interns experience of the work of the Museum, and to enable recipients to apply their academic expertise in working with a relevant area of the Museum collection
Subject: Economic history, numismatics

150 Ford Foundation Grants and Programs

Awarding body: Ford Foundation (USA)
Address: Ford Foundation (Headquarters), 320 E 43rd St, New York, NY 10017, USA
Tel: (001) 212 573 5000
Fax: (001) 212 351 3677
Email: office-secretary@fordfound.org
Web: www.fordfound.org
Contact: Secretary
Award: Various grants available
Objective: For a variety of educational purposes, including conferences and seminars, publications, research and fellowships
Subject: Asset-building and community development, peace and social justice, knowledge, creativity and freedom

151 Griffith Egyptological Fund

Awarding body: Oriental Institute – University of Oxford
Address: Griffith Egyptological Fund, Oriental Institute, Pusey Lane, Oxford OX1 2LE
Tel: 01865 278 2000
Fax: 01865 278 1900
Email: orient@orinst.ox.ac.uk
Web: www.orinst.ox.ac.uk
Contact: Fund Administrator
Award: Awarded termly, deadline Friday of 3rd week of each full term
Objective: To support fieldwork in Egypt, conference attendance to deliver papers, publication costs and research trips to work with collections
Subject: The history and antiquities of Egypt and the Nile Valley and the anthropology of north-east Africa

152 Hellenic Society Council Grants

Awarding body: Hellenic Society
Address: Society for the Promotion of Hellenic Studies, Senate House, Malet St, London WC1E 7HU
Tel: 020 7862 8730
Fax: 020 7862 8731
Email: office@hellenicsociety.org.uk
Web: www.hellenicsociety.org.uk
Contact: Secretary
Award: Value varies but normally £100–£500, open to schools and institutions to fund projects and events
Objective: To assist school and institutional projects concerned with the teaching of Greek or Greek civilisations
Subject: Greece or Greek civilisations

153 Jean Monnet Programme

Awarding body: European Commission (Belgium)
Address: European Commission, DG for Education and Culture, Jean Monnet Programme, Madou, B-1049 Brussels, Belgium
Email: eac-info@ec.europa.eu
Web: http://ec.europa.eu/education/ lifelong-learning-programme/doc88_ en.htm
Contact: Luciano di Fonzon
Award: Funding for teaching, transnational research and conferences/seminars on European integration at university level, closing date 28 Feb
Objective: To increase awareness, knowledge and debate on European integration
Subject: European integration

154 Lifelong Learning Programme: Erasmus
Awarding body: European Union (European Commission)
Address: UK Socrates-Erasmus Council, 28 Park Place, Cardiff CF10 3QE
Tel: 029 2039 7405
Email: erasmus@britishcouncil.org
Web: www.erasmus-uk.org.uk
Award: Support for students
Objective: To encourage transnational co-operation between HEIs and to promote the mobility of students and university staff
Subject: Any subject

155 Metropolitan Museum of Art Internships
Awarding body: Metropolitan Museum of Art (USA)
Address: Metropolitan Museum of Art, 1000 5th Ave, New York, NY 10028-0198, USA
Email: mmainterns@metmuseum.org
Web: www.metmuseum.org/en/research/internships-and-fellowships/internships/
Contact: Internship Programs
Award: Various programmes ranging between 10 weeks and 12 months, for college and graduate students and recent graduates interested in careers in art museums, value varies
Objective: To develop students interested in careers in art museums
Subject: Art history, museum studies or related fields

156 Pasold Research Fund
Awarding body: Pasold Research Fund
Address: Pasold Research Fund, Global History and Culture Centre, Department of History, University of Warwick, Coventry CV4 7AL
Email: g.riello@warwick.ac.uk
Web: www.pasold.co.uk
Contact: Dr Giorgio Riello, Director
Award: Research Activity Grants (up to £750), applications may be made at any time, Research Project Grants (£751–£2,500), closing dates 1 Oct, 1 Mar, PhD grants (up to £2,500), closing date 15 Jun, publication grants (up to £1,000), closing dates 1 Sept, 15 Feb, Raine Grants to assist individual staff working in UK museums (up to £500), closing date 30 Jun
Objective: To fund high quality research relating to all branches of textile history
Subject: Textile history

157 Tomlin Fund
Awarding body: Society for Nautical Research
Address: 6 Ashmeadow Rd, Arnside, via Carnforth, Lancs LA5 0AE
Email: research@snr.org.uk
Web: www.snr.org.uk/pages/research/tomlin-fund/
Contact: Dr Edward Hampshire, Secretary of the Research, Technical and Programme Committee
Award: Value up to £1,500 for expenses incurred during archival research and investigation of maritime history, and in particular maritime technology, survey or research costs relating to historic ships and shipbuilding, conference expenses or publication expenses
Objective: To support research
Subject: Maritime history

158 Wellcome Trust Awards, Fellowships and Studentships

Awarding body: Wellcome Trust
Address: Grants Section (History of Medicine), Wellcome Trust, Gibbs Building, 215 Euston Rd, London NW1 2BE
Tel: 020 7611 8499
Fax: 020 7611 8545
Email: mh@wellcome.ac.uk
Web: www.wellcome.ac.uk
Award: A large number awarded, variable value and closing dates, open to academic staff, postgraduate students and HEIs, see website for full range of awards
Objective: To fund research that will further develop understandings of the impact of medicine and medical sciences on human and animal health
Subject: History of medicine

159 Wolfson Foundation Grants

Awarding body: Wolfson Foundation
Address: Wolfson Foundation, 8 Queen Anne St, London W1G 9LD
Tel: 020 7323 5730
Fax: 020 7323 3241
Web: www.wolfson.org.uk
Contact: Chief Secretary
Award: Number and value varies, offered biannually, online stage one deadlines are 1 Jan and 1 July each year, full details from website
Objective: Awards are generally for capital projects, normally for registered charities and exempt charities, including universities, libraries, museums, galleries, theatres, academies and historic buildings
Subject: Subjects including arts and humanities

6   Postdoctoral awards

160   Alan Pearsall Postdoctoral Fellowship in Naval and Maritime History

Awarding body: Institute of Historical Research (IHR) – University of London
Address: IHR, University of London, Senate House, Malet St, London WC1E 7HU
Tel: 020 7862 8740
Fax: 020 7862 8745
Email: james.lees@sas.ac.uk
Web: www.history.ac.uk
Contact: Fellowships Officer
Award: One offered annually, value approx £22,000, closing date early Apr
Objective: To support postdoctoral research into any aspect of naval or maritime history (broadly defined)
Subject: Naval or maritime history

161   British Academy Postdoctoral Fellowships

Awarding body: British Academy
Address: British Academy, 10 Carlton House Terrace, London SW1Y 5AH
Tel: 020 7969 5200
Fax: 020 7969 5300
Email: posts@britac.ac.uk
Web: www.britac.ac.uk
Contact: Research Awards Team
Award: Up to 45 awarded annually, tenable for 3 years non-renewable, closing date 9 Oct
Objective: To support research of recent postdoctoral scholars, normally within 3 years of obtaining the PhD
Subject: Humanities and social sciences

162   Brooke Hindle Postdoctoral Fellowship

Awarding body: Society for the History of Technology (SHOT) (USA)
Address: SHOT, c/o Department of Science, Technology and Society, University of Virginia, PO Box 400744, Charlottesville, VA 22904-4744, USA
Tel: (001) 434 987 6230
Email: shot@virginia.edu
Web: www.historyoftechnology.org/awards/hindle.html
Contact: Executive Secretary
Award: Value US$10,000, awarded in alternate years, open to doctorates in the history of technology or a related field, to support preparation of a dissertation for publication as articles or as a monograph or to develop a new project based on primary research, closing date mid Apr
Objective: To support postdoctoral research or writing
Subject: History of technology

163   Economic History Fellowships

Awarding body: Institute of Historical Research (IHR) – University of London
Address: IHR, University of London, Senate House, Malet St, London WC1E 7HU
Tel: 020 7862 8740
Fax: 020 7862 8745
Email: james.lees@sas.ac.uk
Web: www.history.ac.uk
Contact: Fellowships Officer
Award: Up to 5 offered annually, value set at research council level, for postdoctoral academics, for 1 year, closing date early Apr
Objective: To support research
Subject: Economic and social history

164   Elie Kedourie Memorial Fund Research Grants

Awarding body: British Academy
Address: British Academy, 10 Carlton House Terrace, London SW1Y 5AH
Tel: 020 7969 5200
Fax: 020 7969 5300
Email: grants@britac.ac.uk
Web: www.britac.ac.uk
Contact: Research Grants Department
Award: Value max £1,000, for recent postdoctoral scholars of any nationality, closing date 15 Mar
Objective: To promote the study of history
Subject: Middle Eastern and modern European history, history of political thought

165   Elisabeth Barker Fund

Awarding body: British Academy
Address: British Academy, 10 Carlton House Terrace, London SW1Y 5AH
Tel: 020 7969 5200
Fax: 020 7969 5300
Email: grants@britac.ac.uk
Web: www.britac.ac.uk
Contact: Research Awards Team
Award: Variable number, grants up to total value of £10,000, apply through British Academy Small Research Grants scheme, closing date 16 Oct
Objective: To support primary research for collaborative or individual research projects
Subject: Recent European history, particularly of east and central Europe

166   Franklin Research Grants

Awarding body: American Philosophical Society (USA)
Address: Franklin Research Grants, American Philosophical Society, 104 S 5th St, Philadelphia, PA 19106-3387, USA
Tel: (001) 215 440 3429
Email: lmusumeci@amphilsoc.org
Web: www.amphilsoc.org/grants/franklin/
Contact: Linda Musumeci
Award: Awarded biannually, open to those with the doctorate or those who have published work of doctoral quality, value up to US$6,000, closing dates 1 Oct, 1 Dec for decisions in Jan and Mar
Objective: To support research leading to publication in all areas of knowledge – foreign nationals must indicate the US-based objects of research to which they need access
Subject: Any subject

167   Harvard-Newcomen Postdoctoral Fellowship

Awarding body: Harvard Business School (USA)
Address: Rock Center 104, Harvard Business School, Boston, MA 02163, USA
Email: wfriedman@hbs.edu
Web: www.hbs.edu/businesshistory/fellowships.html
Contact: Walter A Friedman
Award: Value US$60,000, for 1 year, open to those who have received the PhD in the last 10 years, closing date 15 Oct
Objective: To support postdoctoral study in business history
Subject: Business history

168   Humboldt Research Fellowship for Postdoctoral Researchers

Awarding body: Alexander von Humboldt Foundation (Germany)
Address: Humboldt Foundation, Selection Department, Jean-Paul Strasse 12, D-53173, Bonn, Germany

Tel: (0049) 228 8330
Fax: (0049) 228 833 212
Email: info@avh.de
Web: www.humboldt-foundation.de
Contact: www.humboldt-foundation.de
Award: Monthly fellowship rate of
€2,650 plus research, travel and
family allowances for 6–24 months,
open to highly qualified, early stage
researchers from abroad who
completed their doctorate less than 4
years ago
Objective: To support long-term
research stays in Germany for
academics from outside Germany
Subject: Any subject

169   IASH Postdoctoral Bursaries

Awarding body: Institute for Advanced
Studies in the Humanities (IASH)
Address: IASH, University of
Edinburgh, Hope Park Sq, Edinburgh
EH8 9NW
Tel: 0131 650 4671
Fax: 0131 668 2252
Email: iash@ed.ac.uk
Web: www.iash.ed.ac.uk
Contact: Secretary
Award: For those awarded the
doctorate within the last 3 years, value
max £10,000, tenable at the Institute
for 3–9 months, closing date early
June
Objective: To promote advanced
research in the humanities and social
science
Subject: Research related to the
Institute's research themes or
across disciplinary boundaries in the
humanities and social science

170   IASH Visiting Research Fellowships

Awarding body: Institute for Advanced
Studies in the Humanities (IASH)
Address: IASH, University of
Edinburgh, Hope Park Sq, Edinburgh
EH8 9NW
Tel: 0131 650 4671
Fax: 0131 668 2252
Email: iash@ed.ac.uk
Web: www.iash.ed.ac.uk
Contact: Secretary
Award: Tenable at the Institute for
2–6 months, open to scholars with
a doctorate or equivalent, non-
stipendiary, closing date Feb
Objective: To promote advanced
research in the humanities and to
sponsor interdisciplinary research
Subject: Interdisciplinary research,
including history, history of science
and art history, priority given to topics
related to IASH current research
themes

171 IASH-SSPS Visiting Research Fellowships

Awarding body: Institute for Advanced Studies in the Humanities (IASH) and School of Social and Political Science (SSPS), University of Edinburgh
Address: IASH, University of Edinburgh, Hope Park Sq, Edinburgh EH8 9NW
Tel: 0131 650 4671
Fax: 0131 668 2252
Email: iash@ed.ac.uk
Web: www.sps.ed.ac.uk/research/fellowships/iash-ssps_visiting_research_fellowships/
Contact: Secretary
Award: Tenable at the IASH for 2–4 months, open to scholars with a doctorate or equivalent, non-stipendiary, closing date Feb
Objective: To encourage outstanding research, international scholarly collaboration and networking activities
Subject: Social and political science

172 Leverhulme Trust Early Career Fellowships

Awarding body: Leverhulme Trust
Address: Research Awards Advisory Committee, Leverhulme Trust, 1 Pemberton Row, London EC4A 3BG
Tel: 020 7042 9861
Fax: 020 7042 9889
Email: aheiner@leverhulme.ac.uk
Web: www.leverhulme.ac.uk
Contact: Andreas Heiner
Award: Approx 80 offered for a period of 2–3 years, open to those with a doctorate or equivalent research experience who have not held an established academic post, based on a pattern of joint support with the Trust contributing 50% of salary to a max of £23,000 per annum, closing date 6 Mar

Objective: To provide career development opportunities for those who are at a relatively early stage of their academic careers but with a proven record of research
Subject: Any subject

173 Michigan Society of Fellows Postdoctoral Fellowships in the Humanities, Arts, Sciences and Professions

Awarding body: Michigan Society of Fellows (USA)
Address: Michigan Society of Fellows, 0540 Rackham Building, 915 E Washington St, Ann Arbor, MI 48109-1070, USA
Tel: (001) 734 763 1259
Email: society.of.fellows@umich.edu
Web: http://societyoffellows.umich.edu/
Award: Eight fellowships awarded each year, stipend US$55,000 to individuals selected for outstanding achievement, professional promise and interdisciplinary interests, candidates must have received the PhD or equivalent within the last 3 years, closing date 1 Oct
Objective: To promote academic and creative excellence
Subject: Humanities, arts, sciences and professions

174 Neil Ker Memorial Fund

Awarding body: British Academy
Address: British Academy, 10 Carlton House Terrace, London SW1Y 5AH
Tel: 020 7969 5200
Fax: 020 7969 5300
Email: grants@britac.ac.uk
Web: www.britac.ac.uk
Contact: Research Awards Team
Award: Grants offered annually, number varies, value max £2,000,

open to younger and established postdoctoral scholars of any nationality, closing date 4 Dec *Objective:* For research at the postdoctoral level, to promote the study of western medieval manuscripts, with their production (including decoration), readership and use being particularly relevant aspects *Subject:* Western medieval manuscripts, particularly those of British interest

175 Newby Trust Postdoctoral Bursary

Awarding body: Institute for Advanced Studies in the Humanities (IASH)
Address: IASH, University of Edinburgh, Hope Park Sq, Edinburgh EH8 9NW
Tel: 0131 650 4671
Fax: 0131 668 2252
Email: iash@ed.ac.uk
Web: www.iash.ed.ac.uk
Contact: Secretary
Award: For those awarded the doctorate within the last 3 years, value £10,000, tenable at the Institute for 9 months, closing date 8 July
Objective: To promote advanced research in the humanities and social sciences
Subject: Research related to the Institute's research themes or across disciplinary boundaries in the humanities and social sciences

176 Past and Present Postdoctoral Fellowship in History

Awarding body: Institute of Historical Research (IHR) – University of London
Address: IHR, University of London, Senate House, Malet St, London WC1E 7HU

Tel: 020 7862 8740
Fax: 020 7862 8745
Email: james.lees@sas.ac.uk
Web: www.history.ac.uk
Contact: Fellowships Officer
Award: Two offered annually, value approx £20,000 for 1 year at the Institute, open to postdoctoral candidates who have not held a postdoctoral award previously, closing date early Apr
Objective: For 1 year's postdoctoral study in history
Subject: History, with preference given to candidates who demonstrate a broad interest in processes of social, economic and cultural change as manifested in their particular field of study

177 Pembroke Center Postdoctoral Fellowships

Awarding body: Brown University (USA)
Address: Pembroke Center, Box 1958, Brown University, Providence, RI 02912, USA
Tel: (001) 401 863 2643
Email: donna_goodnow@brown.edu
Web: www.brown.edu/research/ pembroke-center/postdoctoral-fellowships/
Contact: Donna Goodnow
Award: Residential fellowship with a stipend of US$50,000, applicants must be untenured PhDs, 3–4 awarded annually, closing date 5 Dec
Objective: To contribute to the Pembroke Seminar as well as individual research
Subject: Research varies depending on annual theme, topic for 2013–14 is 'Socialism and post-socialism'

178 Pontifical Institute of Mediaeval Studies Postdoctoral Mellon Fellowships

Awarding body: Pontifical Institute of Mediaeval Studies (Canada)
Address: Pontifical Institute of Mediaeval Studies, 59 Queen's Park Crescent E, Toronto, Ontario M5S 2C4, Canada
Tel: (001) 416 926 7142
Fax: (001) 416 926 7292
Email: barbara.north@utoronto.ca
Web: www.pims.ca/academics/mellons.html
Contact: President's Office
Award: Up to 4 fellowships, valued at Can $35,000, open to young medievalists who have finished their doctoral work in the last 5 years, closing date 1 Feb
Objective: For research at the Institute in the medieval field of the holder's choice
Subject: Medieval studies

179 Rhodes Postdoctoral Fellowship

Awarding body: Rhodes University (South Africa)
Address: Rhodes University, PO Box 94, Grahamstown 6140, South Africa
Tel: (0027) 46 603 8055
Fax: (0027) 46 622 8444
Email: research-admin@ru.ac.za
Web: www.ru.ac.za/research/funding/
Contact: Ms Jaine Roberts, Director, Research Office
Award: Value R140,000 pa, plus research or relocation expenses up to R10,000, applicants must hold recently awarded doctorate, duration 1 year with possibility of renewal for 1 further year, closing date 31 July
Objective: To foster existing academic research and scholarly or creative

activities within Rhodes University departments and institutes
Subject: All subjects

180 Rhodes University Andrew Mellon Postdoctoral Fellowship

Awarding body: Rhodes University (South Africa)
Address: Rhodes University, PO Box 94, Grahamstown 6140, South Africa
Tel: (0027) 46 603 8111
Email: research-admin@ru.ac.za
Web: www.ru.ac.za/research/funding/fellowships/andrewwmellonpost-doctoral/
Contact: Ms Jaine Roberts, Director, Research Office
Award: Value R140,000 pa plus allocation of max R10,000, to be used at the discretion of the head of department, for min 1 year, extendable, open to exceptional postdoctoral scholars, closing date 31 July
Objective: To support research and creative activities at the University
Subject: Humanities and social sciences

181 Rydon Fellowship in Australian Politics and Political History

Awarding body: Menzies Centre for Australian Studies, King's College London
Address: Menzies Centre for Australian Studies, King's College London, Strand, London WC2R 2LS
Tel: 020 7848 1079
Fax: 020 7848 2052
Email: menzies.centre@kcl.ac.uk
Web: www.kcl.ac.uk/menzies/
Contact: Secretary
Award: Value £5,000, tenable at Menzies Centre for 1 term, open

to postdoctoral researchers for converting their dissertations into books or to scholars who are engaged in collaborative research with the Menzies Centre staff
Objective: To support research at the Menzies Centre
Subject: Australian politics and political history, topic must be related to Centre's research goals

182   SHOT-NASA Fellowship in the History of Space Technology

Awarding body: Society for the History of Technology (SHOT) (USA)
Address: SHOT, c/o Department of Science, Technology and Society, University of Virginia, PO Box 400744, Charlottesville, VA 22904-4744, USA
Tel: (001) 434 975 2190
Email: shot@virginia.edu
Web: www.historyoftechnology.org/awards/nasa.html
Contact: Executive Secretary
Award: Stipend of US$17,000, to fund 9 months of research, fellows will also have access to NASA archives, open to researchers who have received the PhD or who have completed all doctoral requirements except for the dissertation, closing date 1 Apr
Objective: To promote the study of the history of space technology, including its technical, cultural, social, institutional and personal context, over the 50 years since NASA's founding
Subject: History of space techology, broadly defined

183   Society for Renaissance Studies Postdoctoral Fellowships

Awarding body: Society for Renaissance Studies

Address: Society for Renaissance Studies, Spanish and Latin American Studies Department, University College London, Gower St, London WC1E 6BT
Tel: 020 7679 7121
Email: a.samson@ucl.ac.uk
Web: www.rensoc.org.uk/funding/fellowships/postdoctoral/apply/
Contact: Dr Alexander Samson
Award: Three awarded annually, value £6,000, open to postdoctoral researchers from institutions in Britain and Ireland up to 5 years after award of doctorate
Objective: To support research
Subject: Renaissance studies, including history, art, architecture, philosophy, science, technology, religion, music, literature and languages. The Rubinstein Fellowship is aimed at supporting the study of Italian history and culture

184   Stein-Arnold Exploration Fund Research Grants

Awarding body: British Academy
Address: British Academy, 10 Carlton House Terrace, London SW1Y 5AH
Tel: 020 7969 5200
Fax: 020 7969 5300
Email: grants@britac.ac.uk
Web: www.britac.ac.uk
Contact: Research Awards Team
Award: Value max £2,500, closing date 4 Dec
Objective: To support postdoctoral research by British or Hungarian nationals
Subject: The antiquities, historical geography, early history or arts of those parts of Asia that come within the sphere of the ancient civilisations of India, China and Iran, including central Asia

185 Stetten Memorial Fellowship in the History of Biomedical Sciences and Technology

Awarding body: National Institutes of Health (NIH) (USA)
Address: Stetten Fellowship Committee, Office of History, NIH, 1 Cloister Court, Building 60, Bethesda, MD 20814-1460, USA
Tel: (001) 301 496 6610
Email: cantord@mail.nih.gov
Web: http://history.nih.gov/research/stetten.html
Contact: Dr David Cantor
Award: A year's research experience in residence at the Office of NIH History, postdoctoral, renewable to a max of 24 months, subject to satisfactory progress and funding, stipend US$45,000, closing date 31 Dec
Objective: Seeks to encourage historical research and writing about biomedical science and technology projects funded by the NIH since 1945
Subject: History of biomedical sciences and technology

186 Villa I Tatti Fellowships

Awarding body: Villa I Tatti (Italy)
Address: Fellowship Application Office, Villa I Tatti, Via di Vincigliata 26, 50135 Firenze, Italy
Tel: (0039) 055 603 251
Email: applications@itatti.harvard.edu
Web: www.itatti.harvard.edu
Award: Fifteen residential fellowships offered each year for postdoctoral research in any aspect of the Italian Renaissance, value according to individual need, max US$50,000, closing date 15 Oct
Objective: To support postdoctoral research in any aspect of the Italian Renaissance

Subject: Any field of Italian Renaissance studies: history (including science and philosophy), art history, literature and music

187 Wolfson College Non-Stipendiary Junior Research Fellowships

Awarding body: Wolfson College – University of Oxford
Address: Wolfson College, Oxford OX2 6UD
Tel: 01865 274102
Fax: 01865 274136
Email: sue.hales@wolfson.ox.ac.uk
Web: www.wolfson.ox.ac.uk
Contact: President's PA
Award: Up to 9 research fellowships offered annually (3 years initially, renewable for 3 years), no stipend but weekly allowance for Common Table meals
Objective: To allow advanced study or research at the College, open to those with no more than 3 years relevant postdoctoral experience, preference will be given to those holding a doctorate
Subject: Humanities and social studies

7   Postgraduate awards

188   Ahmad Mustafa Abu-Hakima Bursary

Awarding body: School of Oriental and African Studies (SOAS) – University of London
Address: Registry, SOAS, University of London, Thornhaugh St, Russell Sq, London WC1H 0XG
Tel: 020 7074 509/5091
Fax: 020 7074 5089
Email: scholarships@soas.ac.uk
Web: www.soas.ac.uk/scholarships/
Contact: Scholarships Officer
Award: One offered annually, value £2,000, for 1 year's postgraduate study, closing date 22 Mar
Objective: To support students whose MA courses include studying the history of the modern Arab world
Subject: History of the modern Arab world

189   Arts and Humanities Research Council – Block Grant Partnership 2

Awarding body: Arts and Humanities Research Council (AHRC)
Address: AHRC, Polaris House, North Star Ave, Swindon SN2 1FL
Tel: 01793 416000
Email: enquiries@ahrc.ac.uk
Web: www.ahrc.ac.uk
Contact: See website
Award: Awards held and advertised by certain institutions, open to high calibre students, resident in the UK (full maintenance grant and fees) and EU (fees only), allocations for 5 cohorts of students between 2014 and 2019, for further information contact the relevant institution directly
Objective: To support postgraduate study
Subject: Arts and humanities

190   Arts and Humanities Research Council – Collaborative Doctoral Awards Scheme

Awarding body: Arts and Humanities Research Council (AHRC)
Address: AHRC, Polaris House, North Star Ave, Swindon SN2 1FL
Tel: 01793 416000
Email: enquiries@ahrc.ac.uk
Web: www.ahrc.ac.uk
Contact: See website
Award: Awards held and advertised by certain institutions, open to high calibre students, resident in the UK (full maintenance grant and fees) and EU (fees only)
Objective: To encourage and develop collaboration between higher education institutions and non-academic organisations and businesses
Subject: Arts and humanities

191   BAJS Studentship

Awarding body: British Association for Japanese Studies (BAJS)
Address: BAJS, University of Essex, Wivenhoe Park, Colchester CO4 3SQ
Tel: 01206 872543
Fax: 01206 873965
Email: bajs@bajs.org.uk
Web: www.bajs.org.uk
Contact: BAJS Secretariat
Award: Financial support for postgraduate research students at UK universities who are members of BAJS, closing dates 31 Oct, 30 Apr
Objective: To contribute towards fees, maintenance or fieldwork
Subject: Japanese studies

192 Bernard Buckman Scholarship

Awarding body: School of Oriental and African Studies (SOAS) – University of London
Address: SOAS, University of London, Thornhaugh St, Russell Sq, London WC1H 0XG
Tel: 020 7074 5091
Fax: 020 7074 5089
Email: scholarships@soas.ac.uk
Web: www.soas.ac.uk/scholarships/
Contact: Scholarships Officer
Award: One offered annually, value equivalent to home/EU postgraduate fee, for 1 year's postgraduate study, closing date 31 Jan
Objective: To provide fee remission for home/EU students taking the full-time MA in Chinese studies
Subject: Chinese studies

193 BFWG Charitable Foundation Emergency Grants

Awarding body: BFWG Charitable Foundation
Address: 13 Brookfield Ave, Larkfield, Aylesford, Kent ME20 6RU
Tel: 01732 321139
Email: jean.c@blueyonder.co.uk
Web: www.ffwg.org.uk
Contact: Grants Administrator
Award: For academic year, open to women graduates in the final year of the PhD or DPhil in real need, grants are unlikely to exceed £2,500, closing dates Nov, Mar
Objective: To support postgraduate research
Subject: All subjects

194 BFWG Charitable Foundation Main Grants

Awarding body: BFWG Charitable Foundation
Address: BFWG Charitable Foundation, 43 Fern Rd, Storrington, Pulborough, West Sussex RH20 4LW
Tel: 01732 321139
Fax: 020 7404 6505
Email: jean.c@blueyonder.co.uk
Web: www.ffwg.org.uk
Contact: Grants Administrator
Award: Value max £6,000, for living expenses only, open to women intending to submit their thesis before end of academic year, studying at institutions in the UK, closing date early May
Objective: For research at the doctoral level
Subject: All subjects

195 Birgit Baldwin Fellowship

Awarding body: Medieval Academy of America (USA)
Address: Medieval Academy of America, 104 Mount Auburn St, 5th Floor, Cambridge, MA 02138, USA
Tel: (001) 617 491 1622
Fax: (001) 617 492 3303
Email: speculum@medievalacademy. org
Web: www.medievalacademy.org/ grants/gradstudent_grants_baldwin. htm
Award: Grant of US$20,000 for a dissertation student in a North American university, for 1 year of study, renewable for a further year, applicants must be members of the Medieval Academy, closing date 15 Nov
Objective: To enable sustained research in the archives and libraries of France
Subject: French medieval history

196 Birkbeck Research Studentships

Awarding body: Birkbeck – University of London
Address: School of History, Classics and Archaeology, Birkbeck, University of London, Malet St, London WC1E 7HX
Tel: 020 7631 6268
Email: s.brady@bbk.ac.uk
Web: www.bbk.ac.uk/mybirkbeck/ finance/studentfinance/res_finance/
Contact: Department of History, Classics and Archaeology
Award: Fee waivers and reduced fees, open to full-time and part-time PhD students, closing date 4 Feb
Objective: To support research students at Birkbeck
Subject: History, ancient history and archaeology

197 University of Birmingham College of Arts and Law Scholarships

Awarding body: University of Birmingham
Address: Postgraduate Office, College of Arts and Law Graduate School, University of Birmingham, ERI Building, Pritchatts Rd, Birmingham B15 2TT
Tel: 0121 414 8442
Email: artsandlawgraduateschool@ contacts.bham.ac.uk
Web: www.birmingham.ac.uk/schools/ calgs/
Contact: College of Arts and Law Graduate School
Award: There are a number of awards available, please refer to the funding and scholarships page on the College of Arts and Law Graduate School website
Objective: To support postgraduate research at the University

Subject: African studies, American and Canadian studies, ancient, medieval and modern history, archaeology, Byzantine, Ottoman and modern Greek studies, classics, history of art, theology and religion

198 University of Bristol Postgraduate Research Scholarships

Awarding body: University of Bristol
Address: Student Funding Officer, Student Funding Office, University of Bristol, Senate House, Tyndall Ave, Clifton, Bristol BS8 1TH
Tel: 0117 3317972
Fax: 0117 331 7873
Email: student-funding@bris.ac.uk
Web: www.bristol.ac.uk/arts/ gradschool/financial-aid/
Contact: Student Funding Office
Award: Funding for tuition fees and maintenance for a period of up to 3 years, amounts vary, open to new entrants on full-time PhD research degrees only
Objective: To support research at the University
Subject: All subjects, including history

199 British Association for Slavonic and East European Studies Postgraduate Research Grants

Awarding body: British Association for Slavonic and East European Studies (BASEES)
Address: BASEES, University of Bristol, 17 Woodland Rd, Bristol BS8 1TE
Email: derek.hutcheson@ucd.ie
Web: www.basees.org.uk
Contact: Dr Derek Hutcheson, Research, Development and Study Groups Co-ordinator
Award: Value max £600, for doctoral and MA students who have been members of the Association for more than 6 months
Objective: To support fieldwork or work in libraries and archives, to aid travel to overseas conferences
Subject: East European studies

200 British Chamber of Commerce in Germany Foundation Scholarships

Awarding body: British Chamber of Commerce in Germany Foundation (Germany)
Address: British Chamber of Commerce in Germany e.V., Friedrichstr 140, 10117 Berlin, Germany Meerbusch, Germany
Email: foundation@bccg.de
Web: www.bccg.de
Contact: Frau Christine Hoyer
Award: Support for English and German students who plan to study in the other country, closing date 30 June
Objective: To promote understanding between the peoples and the furtherance of cultural relations between the two countries
Subject: Any

201 British Federation of Women Graduates Awards

Awarding body: British Federation of Women Graduates (BFWG)
Address: BFWG HQ, Mandeville Courtyard, 142 Battersea Park Rd, London SW11 4NB
Tel: 020 7498 8037
Fax: 020 7498 5213
Email: awards@bfwg.org.uk
Web: www.bfwg.org.uk
Contact: Awards Administrator
Award: A number of awards and scholarships offered annually to women PhD students for their third year of doctoral studies at British universities (not Northern Ireland) on the basis of academic excellence, ranging from £1,000–£5,000, closing date late Mar
Objective: To promote academic study and research by women
Subject: Any subject

202 BSHS Master's Degree Bursaries

Awarding body: British Society for the History of Science (BSHS)
Address: BSHS Executive Secretary, PO Box 3401, Norwich NR7 7JF
Email: office@bshs.org.uk
Web: http://bshs.org.uk/grants/masters-degree-bursaries/
Contact: Executive Secretary
Award: Bursaries of £1,000 towards living costs for Master's students, several available, preference may be given to those who have not previously studied history of science, closing date 30 Sept
Objective: To support students taking taught Master's courses in the history of science, technology or medicine
Subject: History of science, technology or medicine

203 CAARI Graduate Student Fellowships

Awarding body: Cyprus American Archaeological Research Institute (CAARI) (USA)
Address: CAARI at Boston University, 656 Beacon St, 5th Floor, Boston, MA 02215, USA
Tel: (001) 617 353 6571
Fax: (001) 617 353 6575
Email: caari@bu.edu
Web: www.caari.org/Fellowships.htm
Award: Several named grants of US$1,000, for graduate students of any nationality, residence at CAARI and to help defray costs of travel, check website for closing date
Objective: To support research on a project relevant to the archaeology of Cyprus
Subject: Archaeology of Cyprus

204 Caledonian Scholarships

Awarding body: Carnegie Trust for the Universities of Scotland
Address: Carnegie Trust for the Universities of Scotland, Andrew Carnegie House, Pittencrieff St, Dunfermline KY12 8AW
Tel: 01383 724990
Fax: 01383 749799
Email: pkrus@carnegie-trust.org
Web: www.carnegie-trust.org
Contact: Secretary and Treasurer
Award: One or 2 offered annually, value £15,200, plus tuition fees, tenable at any Scottish university for max 3 years, open to anyone with a first-class degree from a Scottish university, closing date 15 Mar
Objective: To support postgraduate research
Subject: All subjects

205 Carnegie Scholarships

Awarding body: Carnegie Trust for the Universities of Scotland
Address: Carnegie Trust for the Universities of Scotland, Andrew Carnegie House, Pittencrieff St, Dunfermline KY12 8AW
Tel: 01383 724990
Fax: 01383 749799
Email: rkrus@carnegie-trust.org
Web: www.carnegie-trust.org
Contact: Secretary and Treasurer
Award: Up to 14 offered annually, value £15,200, plus tuition fees, tenable at any Scottish university for max 3 years, open to anyone with a first-class degree from a Scottish university, closing date 15 Mar
Objective: To support postgraduate research
Subject: Any subject

206 Clarendon Fund Scholarships

Awarding body: Clarendon Fund
Address: Graduate Admissions and Funding, University Offices, Wellington Square, Oxford OX1 2JD
Tel: 01865 280487
Email: clarendon@admin.ox.ac.uk
Web: www.clarendon.ox.ac.uk
Contact: Graduate Admissions and Funding, University of Oxford
Award: Award consists of tuition and college fees in full and living allowance of at least £13,726 for full-time students for each year of course, open to new graduate students
Objective: To support academically excellent students with the potential to become leaders in their fields
Subject: Unrestricted

207 Council for European Studies Pre-Dissertation Research Fellowships

Awarding body: Council for European Studies (CES) (USA)
Address: CES, Columbia University, 420 W 118th St, MC 3310, New York, NY 10027, USA
Tel: (001) 212 854 4172
Fax: (001) 212 854 8808
Email: ces@columbia.edu
Web: http://councilforeuropeanstudies.
org/grants-and-awards/pre-
dissertation-research/
Contact: Siovahn Walker, Director
Award: Stipend of US$4,000 to fund 2 months' travel in Europe to conduct exploratory research for a projected dissertation project, opportunity to publish in the Council's journal *Perspectives on Europe* and to participate in the International Conference of Europeanists
Objective: To fund students' first major research project in Europe
Subject: All subjects, must pertain to the study of Europe

208 David Bruce Centre Postgraduate Research and Conference Grants

Awarding body: David Bruce Centre for American Studies – Keele University
Address: David Bruce Centre for American Studies, Research Institute for the Humanities, Claus Moser Research Centre, Room CM0.25, Keele University, Keele ST5 5BG
Tel: 01782 734577
Email: brucecentre@ams.keele.ac.uk
Web: www.keele.ac.uk/davidbruce/
funding/
Contact: Tracey Wood, David Bruce Centre Administrator
Award: Financial assistance to enable Keele postgraduate students to carry out the research necessary for the completion of their theses (MRes/MPhil/PhD) and to attend conferences or colloquia on themes close to their subject of interest, applications considered 4 times a year
Objective: To provide research support for Keele postgraduate students
Subject: American studies

209 David Bruce Centre Visiting Junior Fellowships

Awarding body: David Bruce Centre for American Studies – Keele University
Address: David Bruce Centre for American Studies, Research Institute for the Humanities, Claus Moser Research Centre, Room CM0.25, Keele University, Keele ST5 5BG
Tel: 01782 734577
Email: brucecentre@keele.ac.uk
Web: www.keele.ac.uk/depts/as/
Dbruce/bruce.htm
Contact: Tracey Wood, David Bruce Centre Administrator
Award: Financial assistance for non-Keele PhD students to spend up to 2 months in residence at Keele to conduct research, closing dates 1 Dec, 1 Mar, 1 June, 1 Sept
Objective: To provide research support for postgraduate students from outside Keele University
Subject: American studies

210 Economic History Society Bursaries

Awarding body: Economic History Society
Address: Institute of Historical Research, University of London, Senate House, Malet Street, London WC1E 7HU
Tel: 020 7862 8763
Fax: 020 7862 8745
Email: simon.trafford@sas.ac.uk
Web: www.ehs.org.uk
Contact: Dr Simon Trafford, Training Officer
Award: For postgraduate students to attend the IHR-hosted Introduction to Methods and Sources for Historical Research
Objective: To aid travel (and accommodation where necessary), research and study
Subject: History, esp economic and social

211 Economic History Society Bursary Scheme for PhD Students

Awarding body: Economic History Society
Address: Economic History Society, Department of Economic and Social History, University of Glasgow, Lilybank House, Bute Gardens, Glasgow G12 8RT
Tel: 0141 330 4662
Fax: 0141 330 4889
Email: ehsocsec@arts.gla.ac.uk
Web: www.ehs.org.uk
Contact: Administrative Secretary
Award: Award of £5,000, for PhD students at UK colleges and universities
Objective: To assist postgraduate students
Subject: Economic history, social history

212 Economic History Society Research Fund for Graduate Students

Awarding body: Economic History Society
Address: Economic History Society, Department of Economic and Social History, University of Glasgow, Lilybank House, Bute Gardens, Glasgow G12 8QQ
Tel: 0141 330 4662
Fax: 0141 330 4889
Email: ehsocsec@arts.gla.ac.uk
Web: www.ehs.org.uk
Contact: Administrative Secretary
Award: Up to £500 for postgraduate students, closing dates 1 Nov, 1 Feb, 1 May, 1 Aug
Objective: To assist postgraduate students (Master's and PhD) in UK colleges and universities with travel and subsistence expenses incurred in the undertaking of research
Subject: Economic and social history

213 Ecumenical Patriarch Bartholomaios I Postgraduate Studentship in Byzantine Studies

Awarding body: Hellenic Institute – Royal Holloway, University of London
Address: Hellenic Institute, Royal Holloway, University of London, Egham, Surrey TW20 0EX
Tel: 01784 443791/086/311
Fax: 01784 433032
Email: ch.dendrinos@rhul.ac.uk
Web: www.rhul.ac.uk/hellenic-institute/studying/Grants.html
Contact: Dr Charalambos Dendrinos
Award: To cover tuition fees (UK/EU rate) for 1 year on a taught MA or MPhil/PhD in Byzantine and Hellenic studies at the Institute, closing date 31 Aug
Objective: To support students studying at the Institute
Subject: Late antique and Byzantine studies

214 Erasmus Mundus Programme

Awarding body: European Union (European Commission)
Address: UK Socrates-Erasmus Council, 28 Park Place, Cardiff CF10 3QE
Fax: (0032) 22 92 13 28
Email: EACEA-Erasmus-Mundus@ec.europa.eu
Web: www.britishcouncil.org/erasmus-programmes-erasmus-mundus.htm
Award: Funding for an Erasmus Mundus MA programme or joint doctorate programme, amounts vary from €14,400 to €129,900 total depending on length of programme and student's origin, open to citizens of all countries
Objective: To enhance quality in higher education through scholarships and academic co-operation between Europe and the rest of the world
Subject: Any topic covered by an Erasmus Mundus degree programme

215 European University Institute Doctoral Programme Grants

Awarding body: European University Institute
Address: Practitioner Support, Business Services, Memphis Building, Lingfield Point, Darlington DL1 1RW
Tel: 0845 6020583
Email: eu_institutions@slc.co.uk
Web: www.eui.eu/ServicesandAdmin/AcademicService/DoctoralProgramme/GrantInfo/UnitedKingdom.aspx
Contact: Gemma Dundas
Award: A number of 4-year PhD grants available to students undertaking a PhD in the Department of History and Civilization, value €1,508 per month, apply online, closing date 31 Jan
Objective: To allow students to explore European history
Subject: Any aspect of economic, political, social, cultural or intellectual history from the early modern period through to the 20th century

216 Finnish Studies and Research: Scholarships for Postgraduate Studies and Research at Finnish Universities

Awarding body: Centre for International Mobility (CIMO) (Finland)
Address: CIMO, PO Box 343 (Hakaniemenkatu 2), FI-00531 Helsinki, Finland
Tel: (00358) 206 90 501 (Tue–Wed 1300–1600, Thur 1300–1700)
Email: cimoinfo@cimo.fi

Web: www.studyinfinland.fi
Award: Duration 3–12 months,
monthly allowance of €1,200,
application is through the Finnish host
university, see website for details of
short-term scholarship, closing dates
31 Oct, 30 Apr
Objective: To support postgraduate
studies and research at Finnish
universities in Finnish language
and literature and in Finno-Ugric
linguistics, ethnology and folklore
Subject: Finnish language and
literature and Finno-Ugric linguistics,
ethnology and folklore

217   George of Cyprus and Julian Chrysostomides Bursaries

Awarding body: Hellenic Institute –
Royal Holloway, University of London
Address: Hellenic Institute, Royal
Holloway, University of London,
Egham, Surrey TW20 0EX
Tel: 01784 443791/086/311
Fax: 01784 433032
Email: ch.dendrinos@rhul.ac.uk
Web: www.rhul.ac.uk/hellenic-institute/
studying/Grants.html
Contact: Dr Charalambos Dendrinos
Award: For part- or full-time study on a
taught MA or MPhil/PhD in Byzantine
and Hellenic studies at the Institute
Objective: To support students
studying at the Institute
Subject: Late antique, Byzantine and
Hellenic studies

218   Gerald R Ford Scholar Award (Dissertation Award) in Honor of Robert M Teeter

Awarding body: Gerald R Ford
Foundation (USA)
Address: Gerald R Ford Library, 1000
Beal Ave, Ann Arbor, MI 48109, USA
Tel: (001) 734 205 0554

Fax: (001) 734 205 0571
Email: ford.library@nara.gov
Web: www.fordlibrarymuseum.gov
Contact: Elizabeth Druga, Ford
Scholar Award Co-ordinator
Award: Value US$5,000, closing date
10 Apr
Objective: To support dissertation
research and writing, doctoral
students in political science, history,
journalism, communications, public
policy, foreign relations or American
studies are encouraged to apply
Subject: Any field related to the study
of US political process and public
policy, broadly defined, in the last half
of the 20th century.

219   Gilchrist Educational Trust Grants

Awarding body: Gilchrist Educational
Trust
Address: Gilchrist Educational Trust,
20 Fern Rd, Storrington, Pulborough,
West Sussex RH20 4LW
Tel: 01732 321139
Email: gilchrist.et@blueyonder.co.uk
Web: www.gilchristgrants.org.uk
Contact: Grants Officer
Award: Of modest value
Objective: To support those within
sight of the end of their course facing
unexpected financial difficulties
Subject: Any subject

220   Gordon Aldrick Scholarship

Awarding body: Pembroke College – University of Oxford
Address: Pembroke College, Oxford OX1 1DW
Email: admissions@pmb.ox.ac.uk
Web: www.pmb.ox.ac.uk/Students/Graduate_Students/Scholarships_Awards/Graduate_Scholarships.php#Gor
Contact: Admissions and Access Officer
Award: Stipend of £5,000 per year, renewable for each year of course, open to students undertaking a 2- or 3-year research degree at Pembroke College
Objective: To support postgraduate research
Subject: Chinese cultural history

221   Harry S Truman Library Dissertation Year Fellowship

Awarding body: Harry S Truman Library Institute (USA)
Address: Harry S Truman Library Institute, 500 W US Hwy 24, Independence, Missouri 64050, USA
Tel: (001) 816 268 8248
Fax: (001) 816 268 8299
Email: lisa.sullivan@nara.gov
Web: www.trumanlibrary.org/grants/
Contact: Grants Administrator
Award: Value US$16,000, postgraduate, up to 2 awarded each year, applicants should have substantially completed their research and be prepared to devote full time to writing their dissertation, closing date 1 Feb
Objective: To encourage historical scholarship
Subject: Research on some aspect of the life and career of Harry S Truman or of the public and foreign policy issues which were prominent during the Truman years

222   Henry Belin du Pont Dissertation Fellowship

Awarding body: Hagley Museum and Library (USA)
Address: Center for the History of Business, Technology, and Society, PO Box 3630, Wilmington, DE 19807-0630, USA
Tel: (001) 302 658 2400
Email: clockman@hagley.org
Web: http://www.hagley.org/library-grants/
Contact: Carol Ressler Lockman
Award: Residential fellowship of 4 months, value US$6,500, free housing and office privileges, open to PhD candidates whose research would benefit from use of the research collections, closing date 15 Nov
Objective: To support PhD candidates whose dissertation research would benefit from access to the Hagley Museum's research collections, the recipient will make a presentation at the Hagley based on research conducted and will provide a copy of the dissertation
Subject: History of American enterprise

223   Hoskins Duffield Fund

Awarding body: University of Leicester, Centre for English Local History
Address: Centre for English Local History, University of Leicester, Mark Fitch House, 5 Salisbury Rd, Leicester LE1 7QR
Tel: 0116 252 2762
Email: elhinfo@le.ac.uk
Web: www.le.ac.uk/elh/
Contact: Professor Keith Snell, Head of Centre
Award: Grants of up to £900 to assist postgraduate students in the Centre for English Local History with research expenses and fees

Objective: To support postgraduate study
Subject: English local history

224 Institute for Humane Studies Summer Graduate Research Fellowships

Awarding body: Institute for Humane Studies (IHS) – George Mason University (USA)
Address: IHS, George Mason University, 3301 N Fairfax Dr, Suite 440, Arlington, VA 22201-4432, USA
Tel: (001) 703 993 4880
Fax: (001) 703 993 4890
Email: surf@ihs.gmu.edu
Web: www.theihs.org/summer-graduate-research-fellowships/
Contact: Dr Bill Glod, Program Director
Award: Ten offered annually, value up to US$5,000 for graduate students intending academic careers, deadline mid Feb, invitation only – email to inquire
Objective: To encourage interdisciplinary studies in classical liberal and libertarian thought
Subject: Subjects connected with humane studies and the study of liberty

225 Institute for Medieval Studies MA and PhD Bursaries

Awarding body: Institute for Medieval Studies – University of Leeds
Address: Institute for Medieval Studies, University of Leeds, Leeds LS2 9JT
Tel: 0113 343 3620
Email: medieval-studies@leeds.ac.uk
Web: www.leeds.ac.uk/ims/
Contact: Dr Mary Swan, Director of Studies
Award: To be held by a full- or part-time MA or PhD student at the Institute for Medieval Studies, value £5,000 to cover fees and a contribution towards maintenance, closing date 30 June
Objective: For interdisciplinary medieval studies
Subject: Medieval studies

226 Institute of Historical Research Junior Research Fellowships

Awarding body: Institute of Historical Research (IHR) – University of London
Address: IHR, University of London, Senate House, Malet St, London WC1E 7HU
Tel: 020 7862 8740
Fax: 020 7862 8745
Email: james.lees@sas.ac.uk
Web: www.history.ac.uk
Contact: Fellowships Officer
Award: Seven 1-year fellowships offered: 2 Royal Historical Society (open to all nationalities/academic affliations), 4 Scouloudi (open to graduates of UK universities or UK citizens), and 1 Thornley Fellowship (open to PhD students registered at the University of London), closing date early Mar
Objective: To help those in an advanced stage of the PhD to complete
Subject: History

227 Institute of Historical Research Postgraduate Bursaries

Awarding body: Institute of Historical Research (IHR) – University of London
Address: IHR, University of London, Senate House, Malet St, London WC1E 7HU
Tel: 020 7862 8740
Fax: 020 7862 8745
Email: james.lees@sas.ac.uk
Web: www.history.ac.uk
Contact: Fellowships Officer
Award: Up to 11 offered annually (5 funded by the Friends of the IHR, 5 funded by the Alwyn Ruddock Bequest and 1 funded by Prof David Bates), value £500, open to doctoral students registered at institutions based outside London to cover the costs of undertaking research at the IHR, closing date late June
Objective: To help students based outside London to use the facilities of the IHR and other institutions
Subject: History

228 International Medieval Bibliography Bursary

Awarding body: Institute for Medieval Studies – University of Leeds
Address: Institute for Medieval Studies, Parkinson Building, Room 4.05, University of Leeds, Leeds LS2 9JT
Tel: 0113 343 3620
Email: medieval@leeds.ac.uk
Web: www.leeds.ac.uk/ims/
Contact: Dr Mary Swan, Director of Studies
Award: To be held by an international MA or PhD student at the Institute for Medieval Studies, value £1,500 (paid in instalments), successful applicant will work with staff of the International Medieval Bibliography

Objective: To enable the student to undertake practical work experience in the production of the leading interdisciplinary bibliography of the middle ages
Subject: Medieval studies

229 Jesus College Graduate Scholarships

Awarding body: Jesus College – University of Oxford
Address: Jesus College, Oxford OX1 3BJ
Tel: 01865 279723
Fax: 01865 279769
Email: graduate.administrator@jesus.ox.ac.uk
Web: www.jesus.ox.ac.uk/current-students/jesus-college-graduate-scholarships/
Contact: Senior Tutor
Award: Four offered annually, value £900 per year, open to current graduate members of the College
Objective: To reward academic excellence
Subject: All subjects

230 Jesus College Research/Book Allowances

Awarding body: Jesus College – University of Oxford
Address: Jesus College, Turl Street, Oxford OX1 3DW
Tel: 01865 279723
Fax: 01865 279769
Email: graduate.administrator@jesus.ox.ac.uk
Web: www.jesus.ox.ac.uk/current-students/grants-and-awards/
Contact: Senior Tutor
Award: Every graduate at Jesus College may apply for a research allowance of up to £782 pa, and a book allowance of up to £165 pa
Objective: For research
Subject: All subjects

231 John Crump Studentship

Awarding body: British Association for Japanese Studies (BAJS)
Address: BAJS, University of Essex, Wivenhoe Park, Colchester CO4 3SQ
Tel: 01206 872543
Fax: 01206 873965
Email: bajs@bajs.org.uk
Web: www.bajs.org.uk/funding/john_crump_studentship/
Contact: BAJS Secretariat
Award: Financial support for postgraduate research students at UK universities, closing dates 31 Oct, 30 Apr
Objective: To assist during the final stages of the writing up period
Subject: Japanese studies

232 John D Lees Memorial Bursary

Awarding body: David Bruce Centre for American Studies – Keele University
Address: David Bruce Centre for American Studies, Research Institute for the Humanities, Claus Moser Research Centre, Room CM0.25, Keele University, Keele ST5 5BG
Tel: 01782 734577
Fax: 01782 733316
Email: brucecentre@keele.ac.uk
Web: www.keele.ac.uk/depts/as/Dbruce/funding.html
Contact: Tracey Wood, David Bruce Centre Administrator
Award: A £1,500 bursary, open to all those who have applied for a full- or part-time place on the taught MRes in American Studies (US history and politics pathway only), applicants are asked to submit a piece of academic work of 3,000 words by 1 June
Objective: To further and encourage postgraduate research in matters relating to the history and politics of the United States
Subject: American studies

233 University of Leeds Fee Scholarships

Awarding body: University of Leeds
Address: Postgraduate Scholarships Office, University of Leeds, Leeds LS2 9JT
Tel: 0113 343 4007
Fax: 0113 343 3941
Email: pg_scholarships@leeds.ac.uk
Web: http://scholarships.leeds.ac.uk/
Contact: Postgraduate Office
Award: Available for new UK and EU research students undertaking study for 1-year taught Master's and MRes degrees, contributes to academic fees at UK/EU rate
Objective: To support research
Subject: Any subject

234 University of Leeds Research Scholarships

Awarding body: University of Leeds
Address: Postgraduate Scholarships Office, University of Leeds, Leeds LS2 9JT
Tel: 0113 343 4007
Fax: 0113 343 3941
Email: pg_scholarships@leeds.ac.uk
Web: http://scholarships.leeds.ac.uk/
Contact: Postgraduate Office
Award: Available for new UK and EU research students undertaking full-time or part-time study leading to the degree of PhD, covers fees at UK/EU rate and a maintenance grant
Objective: To support postgraduate research
Subject: Any subject

235   University of Leeds School of History Master's Scholarships

Awarding body: School of History – University of Leeds
Address: School of History, University of Leeds, 30-32 Hyde Terrace, Leeds LS2 9LN
Tel: 0113 343 3610
Email: historypg@leeds.ac.uk
Web: www.leeds.ac.uk/history/prospective/pg/school.htm
Contact: Postgraduate Office
Award: Up to 6 scholarships available annually to applicants for the School's taught or by research MA courses, value home/EU fees and a matching maintenance grant (pro rata for part time students), international scholarship winners can opt to amalgamate the payments as a significant contribution to international fees
Objective: To support students undertaking a Master's degree
Subject: History

236   University of Leeds School of History PhD Scholarship

Awarding body: School of History – University of Leeds
Address: School of History, University of Leeds, 30-32 Hyde Terrace, Leeds LS2 9LN
Tel: 0113 343 3610
Email: historypg@leeds.ac.uk
Web: www.leeds.ac.uk/history/prospective/pg/school.htm
Contact: Postgraduate Office
Award: Up to 4 PhD scholarships available annually, paying Home/EU fees and a matching maintenance grant (pro rata for part-time students), international scholarship winners can opt to amalgamate the payments as a significant contribution to international fees
Objective: To support doctoral research
Subject: History

237   University of Leeds Department of Philosophy Scholarships

Awarding body: Department of Philosophy – University of Leeds
Address: Department of Philosophy, University of Leeds, Leeds LS2 9JT
Tel: 0113 343 3263
Fax: 0113 343 3265
Email: j.m.stevens@leeds.ac.uk
Web: www.philosophy.leeds.ac.uk
Contact: Jenneke Stevens
Award: Open to candidates undertaking a postgraduate course (by research or taught) in the Department of Philosophy, University of Leeds, covers fees at the UK/EU rate and may include a maintenance grant
Objective: To support postgraduate study
Subject: Subjects within the School of Philosophy, including history and philosophy of science

238   Leiden University Excellence Scholarship Programme

Awarding body: Leiden University (The Netherlands)
Address: Leiden University, PO Box 9500, 2300 RA Leiden, The Netherlands
Tel: (0031) 71 527 8011
Email: info@leidenuniv.nl
Web: www.leiden.edu/lexs/
Award: Varying levels of support from a grant of 25% of the tuition fee to full tuition fee minus home fee and an allowance of €10,000 for living costs,

open to non-EEA students starting a Leiden University Master's degree, closing date 1 Oct for Feb intake or 1 Feb for Sept intake
Objective: To support postgraduate study for non-EEA students
Subject: All

239 London School of Economics Funding
Awarding body: London School of Economics (LSE) – University of London
Address: LSE, Houghton St, London WC2A 2AE
Tel: 020 7955 6609
Fax: 020 7955 6099
Email: financial-support@lse.ac.uk
Web: www.lse.ac.uk/financialSupport/
Contact: Financial Support Office
Award: Various awards and scholarships for postgraduate study (MPhil/PhD and MSc/MA)
Objective: To support postgraduate study at the LSE
Subject: All subjects

240 Medieval Academy Dissertation Grants
Awarding body: Medieval Academy of America (USA)
Address: Medieval Academy of America, 104 Mount Auburn St, 5th Floor, Cambridge, MA 02138, USA
Tel: (001) 617 491 1622
Fax: (001) 617 492 3303
Email: speculum@medievalacademy. org
Web: www.medievalacademy.org/ grants/gradstudent_grants_madis.htm
Award: Awards of US$2,000 to defray research expenses, applicants must be members of the Medieval Academy, closing date 15 Feb
Objective: To support dissertation research
Subject: Medieval history

241 Mellon-CES Dissertation Completion Fellowship
Awarding body: Council for European Studies (CES) (USA)
Address: Council for European Studies, Columbia University, 420 W 118th St, MC 3307, New York, NY 10027, USA
Tel: (001) 212 854 4172
Fax: (001) 212 854 8808
Email: ces@columbia.edu
Web: www.councilforeuropeanstudies. org/grants-and-awards/disscomp/
Contact: Siovahn Walker, Director
Award: Stipend of US$25,000 plus assistance for health insurance and candidacy/affiliation fees, fellows will publish in the Council's journal *Perspectives on Europe* and participate in the International Conference of Europeanists
Objective: To assist late-stage graduate students in successfully completing their doctoral degree
Subject: All subjects, must pertain to the study of Europe

242 Melvin Kranzberg Dissertation Fellowship

Awarding body: Society for the History of Technology (SHOT) (USA)
Address: SHOT, c/o Department of Science, Technology and Society, University of Virginia, PO Box 400744, Charlottesville, VA 22904-4744, USA
Tel: (001) 434 987 6230
Fax: (001) 434 975 2190
Email: shot@virginia.edu
Web: www.historyoftechnology.org/awards/kranzberg.html
Contact: Executive Secretary
Award: Value US$4,000, open to doctoral students who have completed all requirements for their doctorate except for the dissertation by 1 Sept of the year the award is made, closing date mid Apr
Objective: To support the writing of a doctoral dissertation
Subject: History of technology, broadly defined

243 Meyricke Graduate Scholarships

Awarding body: Jesus College – University of Oxford
Address: Jesus College, Oxford OX1 3BJ
Tel: 01865 279723
Fax: 01865 279769
Email: graduate.administrator@jesus.ox.ac.uk
Web: www.jesus.ox.ac.uk/current-students/meyricke-graduate-scholarship/
Contact: Carole Thomas
Award: Two offered, open to graduates of the University of Wales who have been accepted by the University of Oxford and Jesus College for a course of graduate study, value £900 pa
Objective: For research
Subject: All subjects

244 Middlesex University Postgraduate Scholarships

Awarding body: Middlesex University
Address: Middlesex University, Hendon Campus, The Burroughs, London NW4 4BT
Tel: 020 8411 6286
Fax: 020 8203 6105
Email: scholarships@mdx.ac.uk
Web: www.mdx.ac.uk/courses/postgraduate/fees_funding/scholarships/index.aspx
Contact: Admissions Enquiries
Award: Limited number, value fees and maintenance
Objective: To support postgraduate study
Subject: Any subject

245 Nikolaos Oikonomides Postgraduate Studentship in Byzantine Studies

Awarding body: Hellenic Institute – Royal Holloway, University of London
Address: Hellenic Institute, Royal Holloway, University of London, Egham, Surrey TW20 0EX
Tel: 01784 443791/086/311
Fax: 01784 433 032
Email: ch.dendrinos@rhul.ac.uk
Web: www.rhul.ac.uk/hellenic-institute/studying/Grants.html
Contact: Dr Charalambos Dendrinos
Award: To cover tuition fees (UK/EU rate) for full- and part-time students for 1 year on a taught MA or MPhil/PhD in Byzantine and Hellenic studies at the Institute, closing date 31 Aug
Objective: To support students studying at the Institute
Subject: Late antique, Byzantine and Hellenic studies

246 Northcote Graduate Scholarships

Awarding body: Northcote Graduate Scholarships
Address: The Britain Australia Society, Swire House, 59 Buckingham Gate, London SW1E 6AJ
Tel: 020 7630 1075
Fax: 020 7828 2260
Email: adm@britain-australia.org.uk
Web: http://britain-australia. org.uk/about/strategic-partners/ northcotetrust/
Contact: The Administration Manager
Award: 2–3 offered annually, value A$23,500 pa, plus return airfare and payment of compulsory fees, tenable at any Australian tertiary institution for up to 3 years, postgraduate, closing date 24 Aug
Objective: To enable students to undertake a higher degree in Australia
Subject: Any subject

247 Pat Macklin Memorial Bursaries in Hellenic and Byzantine Studies

Awarding body: Hellenic Institute – Royal Holloway, University of London
Address: Hellenic Institute, Royal Holloway, University of London, Egham, Surrey TW20 0EX
Tel: 01784 443791/086/311
Fax: 01784 433032
Email: ch.dendrinos@rhul.ac.uk
Web: www.rhul.ac.uk/hellenic-institute/ studying/Grants.html
Contact: Dr Charalambos Dendrinos
Award: For part- or full-time study on a taught MA or MPhil/PhD in Byzantine and Hellenic studies at the Institute
Objective: To support students studying at the Institute
Subject: Late antique, Byzantine and Hellenic studies

248 University of Plymouth – Graduate School Scholarships (PhD)

Awarding body: University of Plymouth
Address: Graduate School, Level 3, Link Building, University of Plymouth, Drake Circus, Plymouth PL4 8AA
Tel: 01752 587636
Email: GraduateSchool@plymouth. ac.uk
Web: www.plymouth.ac.uk/pgfunding/
Contact: Graduate School Manager
Award: Limited number offered annually, for new students, to cover Home/EU tuition fees, tenable for 1 year renewable for a further 2 years (for full-time PhD students) or 3 years (for part-time PhD students), open to UK/EU and overseas students
Objective: For study towards the MPhil or PhD
Subject: Any subject

249 Random House Scholarship

Awarding body: St Catherine's College – University of Oxford
Address: St Catherine's College, Oxford OX1 3UJ
Fax: 01865 271768
Email: college.office@stcatz.ox.ac.uk
Web: www.stcatz.ox.ac.uk/vacancies/ graduate-scholarships-current/
Contact: Academic Registrar
Award: Value £2,000 per annum, tenable for up to 3 years, open to postgraduate students, closing date 14 Mar
Objective: To support postgraduate study in Jewish Studies
Subject: Jewish Studies, with preference given to those studying the Holocaust

250   University of Reading Postgraduate Research Studentships

Awarding body: University of Reading
Address: Faculty of Arts and Humanities, University of Reading, Whiteknights, Reading, Berks RG6 6AA
Tel: 0118 378 7348
Email: j.d.lloyd@reading.ac.uk
Web: www.reading.ac.uk
Contact: Jon Lloyd
Award: Tenable for PhDs in any subject area for 3 years, fees paid at UK/EU rate, annual stipend at level of UK research councils
Objective: To support postgraduate research
Subject: Any subject

251   Richard Chattaway Scholarship

Awarding body: University College London (UCL) – University of London
Address: UCL, Gower St, London WC1E 6BT
Tel: 020 7679 7125
Email: j.fryer@ucl.ac.uk
Web: www.ucl.ac.uk/prospective-students/scholarships/graduate/deptscholarships/history/
Contact: Joanna Fryer, Postgraduate Administrator
Award: Value £2,000, closing date 15 May
Objective: To support MPhil/PhD or MA research
Subject: History of modern warfare from 1870

252   Richard III Society and Yorkist History Trust Bursary

Awarding body: Institute of Historical Research (IHR) – University of London
Address: IHR, University of London,

Senate House, Malet St, London WC1E 7HU
Tel: 020 7862 8740
Fax: 020 7862 8745
Email: james.lees@sas.ac.uk
Web: www.history.ac.uk
Contact: Fellowships Officer
Award: One offered annually, value approx £1,000 for 1 year, open to postgraduates, closing date 1 June
Objective: To support research leading to a higher degree
Subject: Late 15th-century British history

253   Robert Sainsbury Scholarship

Awarding body: University of East Anglia
Address: Sainsbury Research Unit for the Arts of Africa, Oceania and the Americas, University of East Anglia, Norwich NR4 7TJ
Tel: 01603 592498
Fax: 01603 259401
Email: admin.sru@uea.ac.uk
Web: www.sru.uea.ac.uk
Contact: Admissions Secretary
Award: Three years' funding, covering tuition fees and living expenses, with a fieldwork and travel allowance, closing date 1 Mar
Objective: For research leading to the PhD
Subject: Ethnohistory, art history, anthropology, archaeology, arts of Africa, Oceania and the Americas

254 Royal Historical Society Postgraduate Research Grants

Awarding body: Royal Historical Society
Address: Royal Historical Society (RHS Research Funding), University College London, Gower St, London WC1E 6BT
Tel: 020 7387 7532
Fax: 020 7387 7532
Email: royalhistsoc@ucl.ac.uk
Web: www.royalhistoricalsociety.org
Contact: Administrative Secretary
Award: Assistance towards travel and research costs only, for postgraduates, closing dates throughout the year.
Objective: To assist with travel and research costs.
Subject: History

255 Royal Historical Society Training and Conference Bursaries

Awarding body: Royal Historical Society
Address: Royal Historical Society (RHS Training and Conference Bursaries), University College London, Gower St, London WC1E 6BT
Tel: 020 7387 7532
Fax: 020 7387 7532
Email: royalhistsoc@ucl.ac.uk
Web: www.royalhistoricalsociety.org
Contact: Administrative Secretary
Award: For postgraduates, closing dates Nov, Jan, Feb, May, June, Sept
Objective: To assist the attendance of postgraduate students at approved short-term training courses designed to widen or enhance skills in historical research or at conferences or other appropriate meetings relevant to research
Subject: History

256 Sainsbury Research Unit for the Arts of Africa, Oceania and the Americas MA Scholarships

Awarding body: University of East Anglia
Address: Sainsbury Research Unit for the Arts of Africa, Oceania and the Americas, University of East Anglia, Norwich NR4 7TJ
Tel: 01603 592498
Fax: 01603 259401
Email: admin.sru@uea.ac.uk
Web: www.sru.uea.ac.uk
Contact: Admissions Secretary
Award: Various awards available to cover travel, study or fees and living expenses, several offered each year, open to applicants to the taught MA
Objective: To support postgraduate study
Subject: Ethnohistory, art history, anthropology, archaeology, arts of Africa, Oceania and the Americas

257 University of St Andrews School of History MLitt Awards

Awarding body: University of St Andrews
Address: School of History Postgraduate Office, St Katharine's Lodge, University of St Andrews, Fife KY16 9AL
Tel: 01334 462907
Fax: 01334 462914
Email: pghist@st-andrews.ac.uk
Web: www.st-andrews.ac.uk/ history/postgrad/taughtpostgrad/ postgradmlittawards.html
Contact: The Postgraduate Secretary
Award: Up to 7 awards, each covering one year's Home fees, open to students undertaking one of the School's MLitt programmes, closing date 26 Apr
Objective: To support students undertaking one of the School's MLitt programmes
Subject: Any subject available in the MLitt programme

258 St Hilda's College Graduate Scholarships

Awarding body: St Hilda's College – University of Oxford
Address: St Hilda's College, Cowley Place, Oxford OX4 1DY
Tel: 01865 276884
Fax: 01865 288637
Email: college.office@st-hildas.ox.ac.uk
Web: www.st-hildas.ox.ac.uk
Contact: Academic Office
Award: Various scholarships to fund either taught postgraduate courses or DPhil research
Objective: For graduates in humanities and social sciences subjects accepted by St Hilda's
Subject: Any in humanities and social sciences

259 St John's College Benefactors' Scholarships for Research

Awarding body: St John's College – University of Cambridge
Address: St John's College, Cambridge CB2 1TP
Tel: 01223 338612
Email: graduate-admissions@joh. cam.ac.uk
Web: www.joh.cam.ac.uk/ scholarships-studentships/graduate-scholarships/
Contact: Tutor for Graduate Affairs
Award: A number offered annually, value approx £13,500 (maintenance grant) plus fees and contribution towards travel and fieldwork expenses plus attendance at conferences, tenable at the College for 1–3 years, closing date 1 Apr
Objective: To support research
Subject: Any subject

260 Schallek Fellowship and Awards

Awarding body: Medieval Academy of America (USA)
Address: Medieval Academy of America, 104 Mount Auburn St, 5th Floor, Cambridge, MA 02138, USA
Tel: (001) 617 491 1622
Fax: (001) 617 492 3303
Email: speculum@medievalacademy. org
Web: www.medievalacademy.org/ grants/gradstudent_grants_schallek. htm
Award: One-year grant of US$30,000, or awards of US$2,000 to defray research expenses, applicants must be members of the Medieval Academy, closing date 15 Oct
Objective: To support dissertation research
Subject: Late medieval Britain

261 School of Oriental and African Studies Doctoral Scholarships

Awarding body: School of Oriental and African Studies (SOAS) – University of London
Address: SOAS, University of London, Thornhaugh St, Russell Sq, London WCH 0XG
Tel: 020 7074 5091
Fax: 020 7074 5089
Email: as100@soas.ac.uk
Web: www.soas.ac.uk/scholarships/
Contact: Scholarships Officer
Award: Up to 4 scholarships for candidates registering for a full-time research degree at SOAS to cover UK/EU tuition fees and maintenance, closing date end of Jan
Objective: To support doctoral study at SOAS
Subject: Arts and humanities

262 School of Oriental and African Studies Doctoral Scholarships – Faculty of Arts and Humanities

Awarding body: School of Oriental and African Studies (SOAS) – University of London
Address: SOAS, University of London, Thornhaugh St, Russell Sq, London WCH 0XG
Tel: 020 7074 5091
Fax: 020 7074 5089
Email: as100@soas.ac.uk
Web: www.soas.ac.uk/scholarships/
Contact: Scholarships Officer
Award: Up to 8 scholarships (1 for each of 6 subject areas and 2 for overseas students) available for incoming full-time research students, renewable for the duration of registration, covers tuition costs, closing date 31 Jan

Objective: To support research at SOAS
Subject: All subjects

263 Sir Francis Hill Scholarships

Awarding body: University of Nottingham
Address: University of Nottingham, University Park, Nottingham NG7 2RD
Tel: 0115 951 4608
Fax: 0115 846 7799
Email: pg-funding@nottingham.ac.uk
Web: www.nottingham.ac.uk/gradschool/
Contact: Graduate School
Award: Awarded annually, number varies, to cover fees and maintenance for up to 3 years, generally at Research Council rates, tenable at the University, limited to one per School
Objective: To promote research
Subject: All arts and social science subjects including history, but changes annually

264 Sir Richard Stapley Educational Trust Grants

Awarding body: Sir Richard Stapley Educational Trust
Address: The Stapley Trust, PO Box 839, Richmond, Surrey TW9 3AL
Email: admin@stapleytrust.org
Web: www.stapleytrust.org
Contact: Administrator
Award: Value £300–£1,000, for 1 year in the first instance, open to graduate degree students with a first-class degree or a 2:1, aged over 24 on 1 Oct of year of study, all initial enquiries ideally by email, application packs available from early Jan
Objective: To support graduate degree students on approved courses in UK universities
Subject: Any field

265 Society for the Study of French History Research Grants

Awarding body: Society for the Study of French History
Address: Society for the Study of French History, School of History and Archives, University College Dublin, Belfield, Dublin 4, Ireland
Tel: (00353) 1 716 8151
Email: sandy.wilkinson@ucd.ie
Web: www.frenchhistorysociety.ac.uk/bursaries.htm
Contact: Dr Sandy Wilkinson, Secretary of the Society
Award: Twelve annual awards of up to £750, open to postgraduate students of the history of France or its current or former possessions who are members of the Society, closing date mid Mar
Objective: To support research
Subject: French history

266 Stanley Burton Research Scholarships

Awarding body: University of Leeds
Address: Postgraduate Scholarships Office, Marjorie & Arnold Ziff Building, University of Leeds, Leeds LS2 9JT
Tel: 0113 343 4007
Fax: 0113 343 3941
Email: pg_scholarships@leeds.ac.uk
Web: http://scholarships.leeds.ac.uk/
Award: Available for new UK or EU research students undertaking full-time doctoral study in the School of Fine Art, History of Art and Cultural Studies or the School of Music, covers fees at UK/EU rate and maintenance grant
Objective: For doctoral research
Subject: Subjects within the School of Fine Art, History of Art and Cultural Studies or the School of Music

267 Stirling Funding

Awarding body: University of Stirling
Address: Graduate Studies, School of Arts and Humanities, University of Stirling, Stirling FK9 4LA
Tel: 01786 467592
Fax: 01786 467581
Email: ahrcbgpapplications@stir.ac.uk
Web: www.stir.ac.uk/arts-humanities/
Contact: Graduate Studies Administrator
Award: Grants may be available under the School of Arts and Humanities for students accepted for the MSc in International Conflict and Cooperation, the MRes in Historical Research and the MRes in Environmental History, any grants available will be advertised on the School web pages
Objective: To support research in History and Politics
Subject: Historical research, environmental history, international conflict and cooperation

268 T E Lawrence Award

Awarding body: Jesus College – University of Oxford
Address: Jesus College,Turl Street, Oxford OX1 3DW
Tel: 01865 279723
Fax: 01865 279769
Email: graduate.administrator@jesus.ox.ac.uk
Web: www.jesus.ox.ac.uk/current-students/history/
Contact: Senior Tutor
Award: Value up to £5,000, open to any fellow, lecturer, postgraduate or a graduate of the College
Objective: For research
Subject: Medieval history of western Europe, the Mediterranean or the territories of the Crusades

269 Tilburg University Scholarship Program

Awarding body: Tilburg University (The Netherlands)
Address: Tilburg University, Attn: TUSP, PO Box 90153, 5000 LE Tilburg, The Netherlands
Tel: (0031) 13 466 9111
Web: www.tilburguniversity.edu/education/masters-programmes/scholarships/
Award: Partial tuition waiver to reduce the fee to €2,500, plus €5,000 to cover living expenses, open to non-EEA students applying to any MA course at Tilburg University, duration 1 year
Objective: To support postgraduate study at Tilburg University
Subject: All

270 Toshiba International Foundation Graduate Research Studentship

Awarding body: British Association for Japanese Studies (BAJS)
Address: BAJS, University of Essex, Wivenhoe Park, Colchester CO4 3SQ
Tel: 01206 872543
Fax: 01206 873965
Email: bajs@bajs.org.uk
Web: www.bajs.org.uk
Contact: BAJS Secretariat
Award: Two available, value £1,500, open to UK and Japanese nationals, application through academic sponsors, closing dates Oct, Apr
Objective: To support research
Subject: Japanese studies

271 UCL Fees Scholarships for MA Programmes

Awarding body: University College London (UCL) – University of London
Address: UCL, Gordon Square, London WC1E 6BT
Tel: 020 7679 1341
Email: claire.morley@ucl.ac.uk
Web: www.ucl.ac.uk/history
Contact: Departmental Administrator
Award: MA programme fees up to max fee paid by the AHRC, all students applying for MA programme by AHRC deadline automatically considered, up to 3 awarded each year
Objective: To support MA study in UCL's History department
Subject: History

272   UCL History Department Research/ Teaching Studentship

Awarding body: University College London (UCL) – University of London
Address: University College London, Gower St, London WC1E 6BT
Tel: 020 7679 7125
Email: claire.morley@ucl.ac.uk
Web: www.ucl.ac.uk/history
Contact: Departmental Administrator
Award: Fees and stipend equivalent to that paid by the AHRC, holder expected to undertake some teaching in second and third years, Home/EU students only, applicants applying for AHRC studentships automatically considered
Objective: To support a programme of study leading to a research degree in UCL's History Department
Subject: History

273   Western Association of Women Historians Founders Dissertation Fellowship

Awarding body: Western Association of Women Historians (WAWH) (USA)
Address: WAWH Founders Dissertation Fellowship Chair, 3242 Petaluma Ave, Long Beach, CA 90808, USA
Email: cbittel@lmu.edu
Web: www.wawh.org
Contact: Carla Bittel
Award: Value US$1,000, open to members of the WAWH, advanced to candidacy, writing the dissertation at time of application, expecting to receive the PhD no later than Dec, closing date 6 Jan
Objective: To help defray the costs of writing the dissertation
Subject: History

274   William R Miller Graduate Awards

Awarding body: St Edmund Hall – University of Oxford
Address: St Edmund Hall, Oxford OX1 4AR
Tel: 01865 279008
Fax: 01865 279002
Email: college.office@seh.ox.ac.uk
Web: www.seh.ox.ac.uk
Contact: Registrar
Award: Three awarded annually, consisting of free single room for 1 year, with possibility of renewal for a further year, closing date Apr
Objective: For postgraduate study
Subject: All subjects

8 Prizes

275 Abraham Lincoln Brigade Archives George Watt Memorial Essay Contest

Awarding body: Abraham Lincoln Brigade Archives (ALBA) (USA)
Address: George Watt Award Committee, Department of Romance Languages, 102 Friendly Hall, 1233 University of Oregon, Eugene, OR 97403, USA
Tel: (001) 212 674 5398
Email: info@alba-valb.org
Web: www.alba-valb.org/participate/essay-contest/
Contact: Gina Herrmann, Chair
Award: At least 2 prizes of US$250 each awarded annually, essays must be between 3,500 and 7,500 words long, completed to fulfil under- or postgraduate course requirements, must have been produced since Jan 2012, work may be written in English or Spanish, closing date 1 July
Objective: To reward an outstanding original piece of work
Subject: The Spanish Civil War, global anti-fascist political or cultural struggles of the 1920s and 1930s, or the lifetime histories and contributions of Americans who fought in support of the Spanish Republic

276 Alec Nove Prize

Awarding body: British Association for Slavonic and East European Studies (BASEES)
Address: BASEES, Faculty of Humanities, University of Bristol, 17 Woodland Rd, Bristol BS8 1TE
Email: S.F.Hudspith@leeds.ac.uk
Web: www.basees.org.uk
Contact: Dr Sarah Young, Secretary
Award: Value £150, offered annually for scholarly work of high quality

in Russian, Soviet and post-Soviet studies, closing date 15 Sept
Objective: To reward a scholarly work published within the 12 months of the calendar year preceding the annual closing date for nominations
Subject: Russian, Soviet and post-Soviet studies

277 Alexander Prize

Awarding body: Royal Historical Society
Address: Royal Historical Society (Alexander Prize), University College London, Gower St, London WC1E 6BT
Tel: 020 7387 7532
Fax: 020 7387 7532
Email: royalhistsoc@ucl.ac.uk
Web: www.royalhistoricalsociety.org
Contact: Administrative Secretary
Award: Value £250, open to doctoral students in history in a UK institution or those within 2 years of completing a doctorate, for a scholarly journal article or an essay in a collective volume published in the last calendar year
Objective: To recognise an outstanding essay
Subject: History

278 Alfred and Fay Chandler Book Award

Awarding body: Harvard Business School (USA)
Address: Rock Center 104, Harvard Business School, Soldiers Field, Boston, MA 02163, USA
Tel: (001) 617 495 1003
Email: wfriedman@hbs.edu
Web: www.hbs.edu
Contact: Walter A Friedman
Award: Awarded every 3 years to the best work in the field of business history published in the US, as voted on by the Editorial Advisory Board of the *Business History Review*
Objective: To recognise an outstanding book
Subject: Business history

279 American Historical Association Prizes, Fellowships and Awards

Awarding body: American Historical Association (AHA) (USA)
Address: AHA, 400 A St, SE Washington, DC 20003-3889, USA
Tel: (001) 202 544 2422
Fax: (001) 202 544 8307
Email: aha@historians.org
Web: www.historians.org/prizes/
Contact: Administrative Office Assistant
Award: Many prizes, grants and fellowships available, value varies
Objective: To reward the best book in designated fields, or to support research
Subject: History, with more specific eligibility requirements for certain prizes

280 American Society for 18th-Century Studies Graduate Student Conference Paper Competition

Awarding body: American Society for 18th-Century Studies (ASECS) (USA)
Address: ASECS, PO Box 7867, Wake Forest University, Winston-Salem, NC 27109, USA
Tel: (001) 336 727 4694
Fax: (001) 336 727 4697
Email: asecs@wfu.edu
Web: http://asecs.press.jhu.edu/awards.html
Contact: ASECS Graduate Student Conference Paper Competition
Award: Value US$200 for the best paper presented by a graduate student at the ASECS Annual Meeting (Cleveland), up to 2,500 words
Objective: To reward the best paper presented
Subject: 18th-century cultural history

281 American Society for 18th-Century Studies Graduate Student Research Paper Award

Awarding body: American Society for 18th-Century Studies (ASECS) (USA)
Address: ASECS, PO Box 7867, Wake Forest University, Winston-Salem, NC 27109, USA
Tel: (001) 336 727 4694
Fax: (001) 336 727 4697
Email: asecs@wfu.edu
Web: http://asecs.press.jhu.edu/awards.html
Contact: ASECS Graduate Student Research Paper Award
Award: Value US$200, for a research essay of 15–30 pages, submissions must include a letter of recommendation from a mentoring professor, closing date 1 Jan

Objective: To recognise an outstanding research essay, which has not previously been published
Subject: 18th-century cultural history

282   American Society of Church History Prizes

Awarding body: American Society of Church History (USA)
Address: American Society of Church History, PO Box 2793, Santa Rosa, CA 95405-2793, USA
Tel: (001) 707 538-6005
Email: keith.francis@churchhistory.org
Web: www.churchhistory.org/researchgrants.html
Award: Various prizes available for the best books (value US$1,500–$2,000), essays (value US$250–$300) or papers read by independent scholars and postgraduate students (value US$500) in different areas of church history
Objective: To promote research
Subject: Church history

283   Annibel Jenkins Biography Prize

Awarding body: American Society for 18th-Century Studies (ASECS) (USA)
Address: ASECS, 2596 Reynolda Rd, Suite E, Winston-Salem, NC 27106, USA
Tel: (001) 336 727-4694
Fax: (001) 336 727 4697
Email: asecs@wfu.edu
Web: http://asecs.press.jhu.edu/awards.html
Contact: Annibel Jenkins Biography Prize
Award: Awarded biennially, value US$1,000, applicants must be members of ASECS at time of award, book must have a copyright date in previous 2 years, closing date 15 Nov

Objective: To reward the book-length biography of a late 17th- or 18th-century subject
Subject: A late 17th- or 18th-century subject

284   Arthur Miller Centre First Book Prize

Awarding body: Arthur Miller Centre for American Studies – University of East Anglia
Address: Arthur Miller Centre for American Studies, University of East Anglia, Norwich Research Park, Norwich NR4 7TJ
Email: awards@baas.ac.uk
Web: www.uea.ac.uk/ams/amc/The+Arthur+Miller+Centre+Prize/
Contact: The Arthur Miller Centre Prize Committee
Award: Prize of £500 awarded annually to the best first book in American studies from the previous calendar year, closing date 1 Mar
Objective: To recognise an outstanding book
Subject: American studies

285 Arthur Miller Centre Prize

Awarding body: Arthur Miller Centre for American Studies – University of East Anglia
Address: School of English and American Studies, University of East Anglia, Norwich NR4 7TJ
Tel: 01603 597592
Email: awards@baas.ac.uk
Web: www.uea.ac.uk/ams/amc/The+Arthur+Miller+Centre+Prize/
Contact: The Arthur Miller Centre Prize Committee
Award: Prize of £500 awarded annually to the best journal-length article written by a UK scholar or published in a UK journal on an American studies topic, entrants must be members of the British Assocation of American Studies, closing date 1 Mar
Objective: To recognise scholarship in American studies
Subject: American studies

286 Barbara 'Penny' Kanner Prize

Awarding body: Western Association of Women Historians (WAWH) (USA)
Address: WAWH, 3242 Petaluma Ave, Long Beach, CA 90808-4249, USA
Email: lsousa@oxy.edu
Web: http://www.wawh.org/awards/
Contact: Lisa Sousa, Award Chair
Award: An annual award given to honour a book, book chapter, article or electronic media that has been verifiably published or posted in the 2 years prior to the award year and which illustrates the use of a specific set of primary sources (diaries, letters, interviews etc), value US$400, closing date 15 Jan
Objective: To honour the best use of primary sources in a history book
Subject: Women's or gender history

287 British Association for American Studies Ambassador's Postgraduate Award

Awarding body: British Association for American Studies (BAAS)
Address: American Studies, School of Humanities, Keele University, Keele, Staffs ST5 5BG
Email: awards@baas.ac.uk
Web: www.baas.ac.uk/postgraduate/the-ambassadors-awards-2010/
Contact: Professor Ian Bell (i.f.a.bell@ams.keele.ac.uk)
Award: Value up to £1,000 to carry out research or attend a conference in the US, awarded to the best 5,000-word essay on a topic relating to America, separate competition for undergraduates, closing date 14 Jan
Objective: To reward the best essay
Subject: Subject relating to American histories, culture and society

288 British Association for American Studies Book Prize

Awarding body: British Association for American Studies (BAAS)
Address: American Studies, School of Humanities, Keele University, Keele, Staffs ST5 5BG
Email: awards@baas.ac.uk
Web: www.baas.ac.uk/awards/baas-book-prize/
Contact: Professor Ian Bell (i.f.a.bell@ams.keele.ac.uk)
Award: Value £500, awarded to the best published book in American studies from the previous calendar year, closing date 14 Dec
Objective: To recognise an outstanding book
Subject: American studies

289 British Association for American Studies Postgraduate Essay Prize

Awarding body: British Association for American Studies (BAAS)
Address: American Studies, School of Humanities, Keele University, Keele, Staffs ST5 5BG
Email: awards@baas.ac.uk
Web: www.baas.ac.uk/postgraduate/baas-postgraduate-essay-prize/
Contact: Professor Ian Bell (i.f.a.bell@ams.keele.ac.uk)
Award: Value £500, open to postgraduate students registered at UK universities, closing date 14 Jan
Objective: To reward the best essay-length piece of work on a topic relating to US culture and society
Subject: Subject relating to American histories, culture and society

290 BSHS Singer Prize

Awarding body: British Society for the History of Science (BSHS)
Address: BSHS Executive Secretary, PO Box 3401, Norwich NR7 7JF
Email: office@bshs.org.uk
Web: http://bshs.org.uk/prizes/
Contact: Executive Secretary
Award: Biennial prize of up to £300, for an unpublished essay by a young scholar, candidates must be registered for a postgraduate degree or have received one in the past 2 years
Objective: To encourage good quality history of science, written by younger scholars
Subject: History of science, technology or medicine

291 Catherine Macaulay Prize

Awarding body: American Society for 18th-Century Studies (ASECS) (USA)

Address: ASECS, PO Box 7867, Wake Forest University, Winston-Salem, NC 27109, USA
Tel: (001) 336 727 4694
Fax: (001) 336 727 4697
Email: asecs@wfu.edu
Web: http://asecs.press.jhu.edu/awards.html
Contact: ASECS Macaulay Prize
Award: Awarded by the Women's Caucus of the ASECS, value US$350, for the best graduate student paper presented at the ASECS Annual Meeting or a regular meeting held in the previous academic year, closing date 1 Sept
Objective: To reward the best graduate student paper on a feminist or gender studies subject
Subject: Feminist or women's studies in an 18th-century context

292 Chalmers-Jervise Prize

Awarding body: Society of Antiquaries of Scotland
Address: Society of Antiquaries of Scotland, Royal Museum, Chambers St, Edinburgh EH1 1JF
Tel: 0131 248 4133
Fax: 0131 247 4163
Email: grants@socantscot.org
Web: www.socantscot.org
Contact: Managing Editor
Award: Offered biennially (2013, 2015), value £500, closing date 30 Nov
Objective: To reward the best essay, illustrated where necessary, on any subject relating to the archaeology or history of Scotland before AD1100
Subject: Archaeology or history of Scotland before AD1100

293   James L Clifford Prize

Awarding body: American Society for 18th-Century Studies (ASECS) (USA)
Address: ASECS, PO Box 7867, Wake Forest University, Winston-Salem, NC 27109, USA
Tel: (001) 336 727 4694
Fax: (001) 336 727 4697
Email: asecs@wfu.edu
Web: http://asecs.press.jhu.edu
Contact: Byron R Wells, Executive Director
Award: Value US$500, for an essay no longer than 15,000 words that appeared in print during the previous academic year, closing date 1 Jan
Objective: To recognise an outstanding article on some aspect of 18th-century culture
Subject: 18th-century culture

294   Criticos Prize

Awarding body: London Hellenic Society
Address: London Hellenic Society, 'Criticos Prize', Hellenic Centre, 16–18 Paddington St, London W1M 3LB
Fax: 020 8442 7000
Email: jason.leech@criticosprize.org
Web: www.criticosprize.org
Contact: Jason Leech, Assistant Prize Co-ordinator
Award: Awarded annually for an original work on Hellenic culture published in the previous year, value £10,000, closing date 31 Jan
Objective: To reward works by writers, artists or researchers on Hellenic culture
Subject: Anything relating to or inspired by Greece, from ancient times to modern

295   David Berry Essay/ History Scotland Prize

Awarding body: Royal Historical Society
Address: Royal Historical Society (Scottish History Prize), University College London, Gower St, London WC1E 6BT
Tel: 020 7387 7532
Fax: 020 7387 7532
Email: royalhistsoc@ucl.ac.uk
Web: www.royalhistoricalsociety.org
Contact: Administrative Secretary
Award: Value £250, for essays between 6,000 and 10,000 words (excl footnotes)
Objective: To recognise an outstanding essay
Subject: Scottish history

296   Dixon Ryan Fox Prize

Awarding body: New York State Historical Association (USA)
Address: New York State Historical Association, PO Box 800, Cooperstown, NY 13326, USA
Tel: (001) 607 547 1416
Email: c.miosek@nysha.org
Web: www.nysha.org/nysha/ publications/history_prizes/
Contact: Paul D'Ambrosio
Award: US$3,000 prize and assistance with publication for the best unpublished manuscript on New York State history, closing date 1 Feb
Objective: Presented each year to the best unpublished, book-length monograph dealing with some aspect of the history of New York State
Subject: History of New York State

297   The Dorothy Dunnett History Prize

Awarding body: The Dorothy Dunnett Society, Centre for Medieval and Renaissance Studies, University of Edinburgh
Address: The Dorothy Dunnett Society, Centre for Medieval and Renaissance Studies, University of Edinburgh, 55-56 George Square, Edinburgh EH8 9JU
Email: ddprize@ddsoc.org
Web: www.dunnettcentral.org
Contact: Academic Prize Administrator
Award: Value £1,000, open to history students registered for the PhD at a UK university, announcement Sept, closing date 18 Nov
Objective: To promote the study of and research into subjects relating to the works of Dorothy Dunnett
Subject: History, politics, culture and religion of the 11th, 15th and 16th centuries

298   Dr A H Heineken Prize for History

Awarding body: The Royal Netherlands Academy of Arts and Sciences (The Netherlands)
Address: Heineken Prizes, Royal Netherlands Academy of Arts and Sciences, PO Box 19121, 1000 GC Amsterdam, The Netherlands
Tel: (0031) 20 551 0700
Fax: (0031) 620 4941
Email: heinekenprizes@bureau.knaw.nl
Web: www.knaw.nl/en/prijzen/prijzen/heinekenprijzen
Award: Trophy and cash award of US$150,000, offered every other year, nominees should be active scholars who are expected to continue their research activities for at least 10 years whose achievements in the field of history are outstanding and a

source of inspiration to others, closing date 15 Nov
Objective: To reward outstanding scholarly achievement in the field of history
Subject: History

299   *Early Medieval Europe Essay Prize*

Awarding body: Wiley-Blackwell Publishing Ltd
Address: Wiley-Blackwell Publishing Ltd, 9600 Garsington Rd, Oxford OX4 2DQ
Tel: 01865 776868
Email: a.sennis@ucl.ac.uk
Web: www.wiley.com/bw/journal.asp?ref=0963-9462
Contact: Dr Antonio Sennis, Co-ordinating Editor, *Early Medieval Europe*
Award: Prize of £200 worth of Blackwell books for the best article published in *Early Medieval Europe* by a first-time author, the article must be the first by its author to be accepted for publication in a refereed journal
Objective: To recognise an outstanding article
Subject: History

300 Economic History Society First Monograph Prize

Awarding body: Economic History Society

Address: Economic History Society, Department of Economic and Social History, University of Glasgow, Lilybank House, Bute Gardens, Glasgow G12 8QQ

Tel: 0141 330 4662

Fax: 0141 330 4889

Email: ehsocsec@arts.gla.ac.uk

Web: www.ehs.org.uk

Contact: Administrative Secretary

Award: Prize of £1,000, to be awarded biennially, for the best first monograph in economic and/or social history, published within 10 years of the author having been awarded a PhD, only monographs published in English during 2012 and 2013 will be eligible for the 2014 prize, closing date 30 Sept 2013

Objective: To reward the best first monograph in the field

Subject: Economic and social history

301 Fraenkel Prize

Awarding body: The Wiener Library for the Study of the Holocaust and Genocide

Address: The Wiener Library, Institute of Contemporary History, 29 Russell Square, London WC1B 5DP

Tel: 020 7636 7247

Fax: 020 7436 6428

Email: info@wienerlibrary.co.uk

Web: www.wienerlibrary.co.uk

Contact: PA to the Director

Award: Two prizes awarded annually, for unpublished work, category A, for a completed but unpublished book (in English, French or German) by an author who has previously published one or more books, value US$6,000, category B, for a completed but unpublished PhD thesis or equivalent, value US$4,000, closing date end Apr

Objective: Awarded for an outstanding work of 20th-century history in one of the Wiener Library's fields of interest

Subject: History of Europe, Jewish history, the two world wars, antisemitism, comparative genocide and political extremism

302 George Blazyca Prize in East European Studies

Awarding body: British Association for Slavonic and East European Studies (BASEES)

Address: BASEES, Faculty of Humanities, St Matthias Campus, University of the West of England, Bristol BS16 2JP

Email: S.F.Hudspith@leeds.ac.uk

Web: www.basees.org.uk/ blazycaprize.shtml

Contact: Dr Sarah Young, Secretary

Award: Prize of £150, offered annually for a book (in English) of high quality in East European studies, taken to include those countries of Eastern Europe that were formerly under communist rule that were not part of the Soviet Union, open to members of BASEES, closing date 15 Sept for works published in the previous calendar year

Objective: To recognise outstanding contributions to the field of East European studies

Subject: East European Studies

303 George Grote Prize in Ancient History

Awarding body: Institute of Classical Studies – University of London
Address: Dr Benet Salway, Department of History, University College London, Gower Street, London WC1E 6BT
Tel: 020 7862 8700
Fax: 020 7862 8722
Email: admin.icls@sas.ac.uk
Web: www.icls.sas.ac.uk
Contact: Dr Benet Salway
Award: Prize of £3,000 awarded for an original and hitherto unpublished study in ancient history, open to postgraduate students in the University of London who have completed no more than 4 years of full-time research
Objective: To promote the study of ancient history
Subject: Ancient history, preferably Greek or Hellenistic history

304 German History Society Essay Prize

Awarding body: German History Society
Address: Royal Historical Society (German History Society Prize), University College London, Gower St, London WC1E 6BT
Tel: 020 7387 7532
Fax: 020 7387 7532
Email: royalhistsoc@ucl.ac.uk
Web: www.royalhistoricalsociety.org
Contact: Melanie Ransom, Administrative Secretary
Award: Value £500, open to postgraduates registered in UK universities, max length 10,000 words, closing date 2 June
Objective: To reward an outstanding essay
Subject: German history, history of Germanic people

305 Gita Chaudhuri Prize

Awarding body: Western Association of Women Historians (WAWH) (USA)
Address: WAWH, 3242 Petaluma Ave, Long Beach, CA 90808-4249, USA
Email: wawh@wawh.org
Web: www.wawh.org/awards/index.html
Contact: Executive Director
Award: Prize for the best monograph about rural women, from any era and any place in the world, published by a WAWH member, value US$1,000, closing date 5 Jan
Objective: To reward an outstanding monograph
Subject: Women's or gender history

306 Gladstone History Book Prize

Awarding body: Royal Historical Society
Address: Royal Historical Society (Gladstone History Book Prize), University College London, Gower St, London WC1E 6BT
Tel: 020 7387 7532
Fax: 020 7387 7532
Email: royalhistsoc@ucl.ac.uk
Web: www.royalhistoricalsociety.org
Contact: Administrative Secretary
Award: For an author's first solely-written history book, published in Britain within the calendar year, entrants must be scholars normally resident in the UK, value £1,000, closing date 31 Dec
Objective: To recognise an outstanding first book
Subject: Historical subjects, not primarily related to British history

307   Hagley Prize

Awarding body: Hagley Museum and Library (USA)
Address: Center for the History of Business, Technology, and Society, PO Box 3630, Wilmington, DE 19807-0630, USA
Tel: (001) 302 658 2400
Email: clockman@hagley.org
Web: www.hagley.org
Contact: Carol Ressler Lockman
Award: Prize for the best book in business history, with either an American or an international slant, written in English and published during the 2 years prior to the award, particularly interested in innovative studies that have the potential to expand the boundaries of the discipline, closing date 31 Dec
Objective: To reward the best book in business history
Subject: Business history

308   Hemlow Prize in Burney Studies

Awarding body: American Society for 18th-Century Studies (ASECS) (USA)
Address: English Department, Duquesne University, 600 Forbes Avenue, Pittsburgh, PA 15282, USA
Tel: (001) 336 727 4694
Fax: (001) 336 727 4697
Email: engell784@duq.edu
Web: http://asecs.press.jhu.edu/ Weekly%20Announcements/ burneyhemlow.html
Contact: Dr Laura Engel
Award: Value US$250, for an essay no longer than 6,000 words by a graduate student, winning essay will be published in the *Burney Journal*, closing date 1 Sept
Objective: To recognize the best essay on any aspect of the life or writings of Frances Burney or members of the Burney family
Subject: Frances Burney's work

309   Henrietta Larson Article Award

Awarding body: Harvard Business School (USA)
Address: Rock Center 104, Harvard Business School, Soldiers Field, Boston, MA 02163, USA
Email: wfriedman@hbs.edu
Web: www.hbs.edu
Contact: Walter A Friedman
Award: Awarded every year to the best article in the *Business History Review*, as voted on by the Editorial Advisory Board of the *Business History Review*
Objective: To recognise an outstanding journal article
Subject: Business history

310   Ivan Morris Memorial Prize

Awarding body: British Association for Japanese Studies (BAJS)
Address: BAJS, University of Essex, Colchester CO4 3SQ
Tel: 01206 872543
Fax: 01206 873965
Email: bajs@bajs.org.uk
Web: www.bajs.org.uk
Contact: BAJS Secretariat
Award: Value up to £400, for essays not more than 20,000 words in length and written within the previous 18 months
Objective: To reward the best essays in Japanese studies
Subject: Japanese studies

311 The Joan Mervyn Hussey Prize in Byzantine Studies

Awarding body: Hellenic Institute – Royal Holloway, University of London
Address: Hellenic Institute, Royal Holloway, University of London, Egham, Surrey TW20 0EX
Tel: 01784 443791/086/311
Fax: 01784 433032
Email: ch.dendrinos@rhul.ac.uk
Web: www.rhul.ac.uk/hellenic-institute/studying/Grants.html
Contact: Dr Charalambos Dendrinos
Award: £500 awarded to Hellenic Institute students who complete the taught MA in Late Antique and Byzantine Studies with the mark of distinction
Objective: To support students studying at the Institute
Subject: Late antique and Byzantine studies

312 John Ben Snow Prize

Awarding body: North American Conference on British Studies (NACBS) (USA)
Address: Professor Ken MacMillan, Department of History, University of Calgary, 2500 University Drive NW, Calgary, Alberta, Canada T2N 1N4
Email: macmillk@ucalgary.ca
Web: www.nacbs.org/prizes/john-ben-snow-prize/
Contact: Chair, NACBS John Ben Snow Prize Committee
Award: US$500 award given annually, deadline 1 Apr
Objective: To reward the best book by a North American scholar on any aspect of British studies from the middle ages to the 18th century
Subject: British history

313 John Leyerle-CARA Prize for Dissertation Research

Awarding body: Medieval Academy of America (USA)
Address: Centre for Medieval Studies, Lillian Massey Building, University of Toronto, 125 Queen's Park 3rd Floor E, Toronto, ON M5S 2C7, Canada
Tel: (001) 617 491 1622
Fax: (001) 617 492 3303
Email: speculum@medievalacademy.org
Web: www.medievalacademy.org/grants/gradstudent_grants_leyerle.htm
Contact: The Director
Award: Annual prize of US$1,000, closing date 31 Jan
Objective: To support the doctoral research of a Medieval Academy member who needs to consult materials available in Toronto collections
Subject: Medieval studies

314 John Nicholas Brown Prize

Awarding body: Medieval Academy of America (USA)
Address: Medieval Academy of America, 104 Mount Auburn St, 5th Floor, Cambridge, MA 02138, USA
Tel: (001) 617 491 1622
Fax: (001) 617 492 3303
Email: speculum@medievalacademy.org
Web: www.medievalacademy.org/grants/gradstudent_cara_brown.htm
Award: Prize of US$1,000 awarded annually for a first book or monograph on a medieval subject, closing date 15 Oct
Subject: Medieval history

315 The John Penrose Barron Prize in Hellenic Studies

Awarding body: Hellenic Institute –
Royal Holloway, University of London
Address: Hellenic Institute, Royal
Holloway, University of London,
Egham, Surrey TW20 0EX
Tel: 01784 443791/086/311
Fax: 01784 433032
Email: ch.dendrinos@rhul.ac.uk
Web: www.rhul.ac.uk/hellenic-institute/
studying/Grants.html
Contact: Dr Charalambos Dendrinos
Award: £250 awarded to Hellenic
Institute students who complete the
taught MA in Hellenic Studies with the
mark of distinction
Objective: To support students
studying at the Institute
Subject: Hellenic studies

316 Judith Lee Ridge Article Prize

Awarding body: Western Association
of Women Historians (WAWH) (USA)
Address: Judith Lee Ridge Prize
Chair, History Department, Cal State
University Sacramento, 6000 J Street,
Sacramento, CA 95819-6059, USA
Tel: (001) 916 278 5636
Email: rkluchin@csus.edu
Web: www.wawh.org
Contact: Judith Lee Ridge Prize Chair
Award: Open to members, primarily
for women historians based in the
western USA, value US$250, closing
date 5 Jan
Objective: To recognise an article
published by a member during the
previous year
Subject: History

317 Julian Corbett Prize in Modern Naval History

Awarding body: Institute of Historical
Research (IHR) – University of
London
Address: IHR, University of London,
Senate House, Malet St, London
WC1E 7HU
Tel: 020 7862 8740
Fax: 020 7862 8745
Email: james.lees@sas.ac.uk
Web: www.history.ac.uk
Contact: Fellowships Officer
Award: Awarded annually by the
Academic Trust Funds Committee,
value £1,000, closing date 1 Oct
Objective: For work not previously
published and based on original
materials
Subject: Modern naval history

318 Kerr History Prize

Awarding body: New York State
Historical Association (USA)
Address: New York State Historical
Association, PO Box 800,
Cooperstown, NY 13326, USA
Tel: (001) 607 547 1480
Email: mason@nysha.org
Web: www.nysha.org/nysha/
publications/history_prizes/
Contact: Catherine Mason, Asst Editor
Award: US$1,000 prize awarded each
year for the best article published in
New York History
Objective: To reward the best article
dealing with some aspect of the
history of New York State
Subject: History of New York State

319   Lavinia L Dock Award

Awarding body: American Association for the History of Nursing (AAHN) (USA)
Address: AAHN, Attn: Dock Award, 10200 W 44th Ave, Suite 304, Wheat Ridge, CO 80033, USA
Tel: (001) 303 422 2685
Fax: (001) 303 422 8894
Email: aahn@aahn.org
Web: www.aahn.org/awards.html
Award: Awarded to a book based on original historical research related to the history of nursing, written in English and in the last 3 years, closing date 15 May
Objective: To recognise outstanding research and writing
Subject: History of nursing

320   Louis Gottschalk Prize

Awarding body: American Society for 18th-Century Studies (ASECS) (USA)
Address: ASECS, 2598 Reynolda Rd, Suite C, Winston-Salem, NC 27106, USA
Tel: (001) 336 727 4694
Fax: (001) 336 727 4697
Email: asecs@wfu.edu
Web: http://asecs.press.jhu.edu/
Contact: Louis Gottschalk Prize
Award: Awarded annually, value US$1,000, applicants must be members of ASECS at time of award, closing date 15 Nov (books must have a copyright date during previous academic year)
Objective: To recognise an outstanding historical or critical study on a subject of 18th-century relevance
Subject: 18th-century history

321   Marc Raeff Book Prize

Awarding body: Eighteenth-Century Russian Studies Association (ECRSA) (USA)
Address: Duke University, International & Area Studies Department, 230 Bostock Library, Box 90195, Durham NC 27708-0195, USA
Email: ernest.zitser@duke.edu
Web: www.ecrsa.org
Contact: Ernest Zitser, President, ECRSA
Award: Cash prize awarded for a book published in previous 2 years, closing date 15 July
Objective: To recognise a publication of exceptional merit and lasting significance for understanding Imperial Russia, particularly during the long 18th century
Subject: 18th-century Russia

322   Mary Adelaide Nutting Award

Awarding body: American Association for the History of Nursing (AAHN) (USA)
Address: 1921 Foulkeways, Gwynedd, PA 19436, USA
Tel: (001) 303 422 2685
Fax: (001) 303 422 8894
Email: lynaugh@nursing.upenn.edu
Web: www.aahn.org/awards.html
Contact: Joan E Lynaugh
Award: Awarded to a postdoctoral research manuscript or article, closing date 15 May
Objective: To recognise outstanding research and writing produced by an experienced scholar
Subject: History of nursing

323   Mary M Roberts Award

Awarding body: American Association for the History of Nursing (AAHN) (USA)
Address: 10200 W 44th Avenue, Suite 304, Wheat Ridge, CO80033, USA
Tel: (001) 303 422 2685
Fax: (001) 303 422 8894
Email: aahn@aahn.org
Web: www.aahn.org/awards.html
Contact: Dr Barbara Brodie
Award: Awarded for original research and writing in an edited book, closing date 15 May
Objective: To recognise outstanding original research and writing
Subject: History of nursing

324   Michael Nicholson Thesis Prize

Awarding body: British International Studies Association
Address: International Politics Building, University of Aberystwyth, Penglais, Aberystwyth, Ceredigion SY23 3FE
Email: theo.farrell@gmail.com *or* bisa@aber.ac.uk
Web: www.bisa.ac.uk
Contact: Theo Farrell, Research Sub-Committee Chair
Award: Prize of £250 for the best doctoral thesis in international studies, to be nominated by awarding department, closing date 15 Jan
Objective: To support the work of new scholars
Subject: International studies

325   *Midland History* Prize

Awarding body: Midland History – University of Birmingham
Address: Midland History, Departments of Medieval and Modern History, University of Birmingham, Birmingham B15 2TT

Tel: 0121 414 5764
Email: midlandhistory@bham.ac.uk
Web: www.maney.co.uk/index.php/journals/mdh/
Contact: Richard Cust
Award: Prize of £250 for the best essay, must be a genuine work of original research, not hitherto published or accepted for publication, for scholars publishing for the first time, winning essay will be published in *Midland History*, closing date 31 Oct
Objective: To encourage research
Subject: Historical subjects relating to midland England

326   Mitchell Prize for Research on Early British Serials

Awarding body: Bibliographic Association of America (USA)
Address: Bibliographical Society of America, PO Box 1537, Lenox Hill Station, New York, NY 10021, USA
Email: bsa@bibsocamer.org
Web: www.bibsocamer.org
Contact: Executive Secretary
Award: Prize of US$1,000 plus a year's membership of the Society, for bibliographical research into 18th-century British periodicals, works published after 31 Dec 2009 will be considered, closing date 30 Sept 2014
Objective: To encourage scholars engaged in bibliographical scholarship on 18th-century periodicals published within the British Isles and its colonies and former colonies
Subject: Bibliographical history

327 Murray Prize for History

Awarding body: Society of Antiquaries of Scotland
Address: Society of Antiquaries of Scotland, Royal Museum, Chambers St, Edinburgh EH1 1JF
Tel: 0131 248 4133
Fax: 0131 247 4163
Email: grants@socantscot.org
Web: www.socantscot.org
Contact: Managing Editor
Award: Biennial prize of £200 and a medal, closing date 1 Nov
Objective: To reward the best original research published by the Society in the *Proceedings of the Society of Antiquaries of Scotland*
Subject: History of Scotland in the medieval and/or early modern periods (*c.* AD 500 to AD 1700), set within a British and/or European context

328 Organization of American Historians Awards

Awarding body: Organization of American Historians (OAH) (USA)
Address: OAH, 112 N Bryan Ave, Bloomington, IN 47408-4199, USA
Tel: (001) 812 855 7311
Web: www.oah.org/awards/
Contact: Award and Prize Co-ordinator
Award: Various awards and prizes, number and value vary
Objective: To recognise scholarly and professional achievement, and to support research
Subject: Primarily American history

329 Oscar Kenshur Book Prize

Awarding body: Center for Eighteenth-Century Studies at Indiana University (ASECS) (USA)
Address: ASECS, 2598 Reynolda Road, Wake Forest University, Winston-Salem, NC 27106, USA
Email: favretm@indiana.edu
Contact: Professor Mary Favret, Director of the Center for Eighteenth-Century Studies at Indiana University
Award: Prize of US$1,000 plus workshop to discuss the book, closing date 31 Jan
Objective: To reward an outstanding monograph of interest to 18th-century scholars working in a range of disciplines
Subject: 18th-century studies

330 The Pollard Prize (sponsored by Wiley-Blackwell)

Awarding body: Institute of Historical Research (IHR) – University of London
Address: The Editor, *Historical Research* (Pollard Prize), IHR, University of London, Senate House, London WC1E 7HU
Email: jane.winters@sas.ac.uk
Web: http://www.history.ac.uk/fellowships/pollard-prize/
Contact: The Editor, *Historical Research* (Pollard Prize)
Award: Awarded annually for the best paper presented at an IHR seminar by a postgraduate student or by a researcher within one year of completing the PhD, publication in *Historical Research* and £200 of Blackwell books, variable number of runner-up prizes offered, closing date end May
Objective: To reward outstanding postgraduate research and writing
Subject: History

331   Rooke Memorial Prize

Awarding body: British-Italian Society/ Society for Italian Studies
Address: The British-Italian Society, 7 Hanover Rd, London NW10 3DJ
Tel: 020 8451 6032
Email: elisabetta@british-italian.org
Web: www.british-italian.org *and* www.sis.ac.uk
Contact: Elisabetta Murgia *and* Dr Charles Burdett
Award: Prize of £350 to 2 undergraduate entrants and £500 to a postgraduate entrant, for an essay or a chapter from a postgraduate dissertation, closing date 30 June
Objective: To raise the profile of Italian studies in UK universities
Subject: Humanities and social sciences relating to Italy, from the middle ages to the present day

332   Royal Historical Society/*History Today* Prize

Awarding body: Royal Historical Society
Address: Royal Historical Society (*History Today* Prize), University College London, Gower St, London WC1E 6BT
Tel: 020 7387 7532
Fax: 020 7387 7532
Email: royalhistsoc@ucl.ac.uk
Web: www.royalhistoricalsociety.org
Contact: Administrative Secretary
Award: Value £250, for an outstanding undergraduate dissertation, 1 entry per history department in UK universities, entry via department only
Objective: To reward an outstanding undergraduate dissertation
Subject: History

333   Sean W Dever Memorial Prize

Awarding body: W F Albright Institute of Archaeological Research (USA)
Address: W F Albright Institute, PO Box 40151, Philadelphia, PA 19106, USA
Email: cardillo@sas.upenn.edu
Web: www.aiar.org/fellowships.html
Contact: Mr Sam Cardillo
Award: Value US$650, for the best published article or conference paper by a PhD candidate, closing date 31 Dec
Objective: To reward the best work in the field
Subject: Syro-Palestinian or biblical archaeology

334   Sheldon Memorial Trust Essay Prize

Awarding body: Sheldon Memorial Trust
Address: Sheldon Memorial Trust, 21 School Lane, Copmanthorpe, York YO23 3SQ
Tel: 01904 705530
Web: www.sheldonmemorialtrust.org.uk
Contact: Trust Secretary
Award: Value £500 (first prize), for an essay on any subject that falls within the objects of the Trust, closing date end July
Objective: To reward an exceptional unpublished essay
Subject: History, literature or the arts in connection with the City of York

335   Sir John Neale Prize in Tudor History

Awarding body: Institute of Historical Research (IHR) – University of London
Address: IHR, University of London, Senate House, Malet St, London WC1E 7HU
Tel: 020 7862 8740
Email: james.lees@sas.ac.uk
Web: www.history.ac.uk/fellowships/awards#neale
Contact: James Lees
Award: Awarded annually to a historian in the early stages of his or her career for an essay of no more than 8,000 words including footnotes, on a theme related to Tudor history, value £1,000 with an additional payment of £500 in support of the development of the prize-winner's scholarly career, normally in the form of research and/or travel expenses and conference attendance, closing date mid Apr
Objective: To reward the best research in the field
Subject: History, 16th-century England

336   Stansky Book Prize

Awarding body: North American Conference on British Studies (NACBS) (USA)
Address: Department of History, California State University, Northridge, 18111 Nordhoff St, Northridge, CA 91330-8250, USA
Email: jeffrey.auerbach@csun.edu
Web: www.nacbs.org/prizes/albion-book-prize
Contact: Professor Jeffrey Auerbach, Chair, NACBS Stansky Prize Committee
Award: US$500 award given annually, deadline 1 Apr

Objective: To reward the best book by a North American scholar on any aspect of British studies since 1800
Subject: British history

337   Susan Strange Book Prize

Awarding body: British International Studies Association
Address: International Politics Building, University of Aberystwyth, Penglais, Aberystwyth, Ceredigion SY23 3FE
Email: bisa@aber.ac.uk
Web: www.bisa.ac.uk
Contact: Gail Birkett, BISA Administrator
Award: Prize of £500 for the best book published in international studies during the last calendar year, to be nominated through recognised BISA Working Groups, closing date 15 Jan
Objective: To recognise the best current work being conducted by members of BISA
Subject: International studies

338   Teresa E Christy Award

Awarding body: American Association for the History of Nursing (AAHN) (USA)
Address: 103 Surrey Rd, Charlottesville, VA 22901, USA
Tel: (001) 303 422 2685
Fax: (001) 303 422 8894
Email: aahn@aahn.org
Web: www.aahn.org/awards.html
Contact: Dr Barbara Brodie
Award: Awarded for doctoral work, typically dissertations, closing date 15 May, AAHN members only
Objective: To encourage new nursing history investigators
Subject: History of nursing

339   Thirsk-Feinstein PhD Dissertation Prize

Awarding body: Economic History Society
Address: Economic History Society, Department of Economic and Social History, University of Glasgow, Lilybank House, Bute Gardens, Glasgow G12 8QQ
Tel: 0141 330 4662
Fax: 0141 330 4889
Email: ehsocsec@arts.gla.ac.uk
Web: www.ehs.org.uk
Contact: Administrative Secretary
Award: Annual prize of £1,000 for the best doctoral dissertation in economic and/or social history, eligible candidates can be nominated by the dissertation supervisor or an examiner, all dissertations must be written in English and must have been awarded during the calendar year preceding the prize, closing date 31 Dec
Objective: To reward the best doctoral dissertation in the field
Subject: Economic and social history

340   T S Ashton Prize

Awarding body: Economic History Society
Address: Economic History Society, Department of Economic and Social History, University of Glasgow, Lilybank House, Bute Gardens, Glasgow G12 8QQ
Tel: 0141 330 4662
Fax: 0141 330 4889
Email: ehsocsec@arts.gla.ac.uk
Web: www.ehs.org.uk
Contact: Administrative Secretary
Award: Awarded at alternate annual conferences, value £1,500 for the best article by a new scholar accepted for publication in the *Economic History Review* in the previous 2 calendar years

Objective: To reward the best article in the field by a scholar within 5 years of receiving the PhD or with no prior publication in the field
Subject: History, especially economic and social

341   Van Courtlandt Elliott Prize

Awarding body: Medieval Academy of America (USA)
Address: Medieval Academy of America, 104 Mount Auburn St, 5th Floor, Cambridge, MA 02138, USA
Tel: (001) 617 491 1622
Fax: (001) 617 492 3303
Email: speculum@medievalacademy.org
Web: www.medievalacademy.org/grants/gradstudent_elliottprize.htm
Award: Prize of US$500 awarded annually for a first article on a medieval subject, author must be resident in the USA, closing date 15 Oct
Objective: To reward an outstanding article
Subject: Medieval history

342   Walter D Love Prize

Awarding body: North American Conference on British Studies (NACBS) (USA)
Address: Professor Sandra den Otter, Department of History, Queen's University, Kingston ON, Canada, K7L 3N6
Email: inazb@uic.edu
Web: www.nacbs.org/prizes.html
Contact: Chair, NACBS Love Prize Committee
Award: US$150 award given annually, deadline 1 Apr
Objective: To reward the best article or paper of similar length or scope by a North American scholar in the field of British history published during the calendar year
Subject: British history

343   Whitfield Prize

Awarding body: Royal Historical Society
Address: Royal Historical Society (Whitfield Prize), University College London, Gower St, London WC1E 6BT
Tel: 020 7387 7532
Fax: 020 7387 7532
Email: royalhistsoc@ucl.ac.uk
Web: www.royalhistoricalsociety.org
Contact: Administrative Secretary
Award: Value £1,000, for an author's first solely-written history book, published in the UK or the Republic of Ireland during the calendar year
Objective: To recognise an outstanding new book on British history
Subject: British history

344   Wolfson History Prize

Awarding body: Wolfson Foundation
Address: Wolfson Foundation, 8 Queen Anne St, London W1G 9LD
Tel: 020 7323 5730
Fax: 020 7323 3241
Email: james.randall@wolfson.org.uk
Web: www.wolfson.org.uk
Contact: Prize Administrator
Award: Prizes awarded annually, usually for 2 exceptional works published during the year
Objective: To promote and encourage standards of excellence in the writing of history for the general public
Subject: History

9   Publications grants

345   Barbara Thom Postdoctoral Fellowships

Awarding body: Huntington Library, Art Collections and Botanical Gardens (USA)
Address: Committee on Fellowships, The Huntington, 1151 Oxford Rd, San Marino, CA 91108, USA
Tel: (001) 626 405 2194
Email: cpowell@huntington.org
Web: www.huntington.org
Contact: Chair
Award: Value US$50,000, for 9–12 months' residence, open to untenured faculty, closing date 15 Nov
Objective: To support the revision of dissertations for publication
Subject: British and American literature, history, art history and history of science and medicine

346   Canterbury Historical and Archaeological Society Research and Publications Grant

Awarding body: Canterbury Historical and Archaeological Society
Address: Canterbury Historical and Archaeological Society, 3 Little Meadow, Upper Harbledown, Canterbury, Kent CT2 9BD
Tel: 01227 760400
Contact: Mrs C M Short, Hon Sec of Grants Committee
Award: Offered annually, value max £500, closing date 30 June
Objective: To support research and publication
Subject: The archaeology and local history of the Canterbury district

347   Harry S Truman Library Scholar's Award

Awarding body: Harry S Truman Library Institute (USA)
Address: Harry S Truman Library Institute, 500 W US Hwy 24, Independence, MO 64050, USA
Tel: (001) 816 268 8248
Fax: (001) 816 268 8299
Email: sullivan.hstli@gmail.com
Web: www.trumanlibrary.org/grants/
Contact: Grants Administrator
Award: Value up to US$30,000, awarded biennially to postdoctoral scholars, closing date 15 Dec in odd-numbered years
Objective: Intended to free a scholar from teaching or other employment for a substantial period resulting in the publication of a book-length manuscript
Subject: Research on some aspect of the life and career of Harry S Truman or of the public and foreign policy issues which were prominent during the Truman years

348   Historic Society of Lancashire and Cheshire Publication Grants

Awarding body: Historic Society of Lancashire and Cheshire
Address: Historic Society of Lancashire and Cheshire, School of History, University of Liverpool, Liverpool L69 3BX
Web: www.hslc.org.uk
Contact: Dr D E Ascott
Award: Grants of up to £1,000 to support the preparation of a publication, closing date 31 Oct
Objective: Grants will usually be made to assist with some specific aspect of the publication
Subject: History or archaeology of Lancashire or Cheshire

349   Hugh Last and Donald Atkinson Funds

Awarding body: Roman Society
Address: Roman Society, Senate House, Malet St, London WC1E 7HU
Tel: 020 7862 8727
Fax: 020 7862 8728
Email: office@romansociety.org
Web: www.romansociety.org
Contact: Secretary
Award: Value £400–£1,500, offered annually, postgraduate or postdoctoral, closing date 15 Jan
Objective: To assist in undertaking, completing or publishing work that relates to the scholarly purposes of the Society
Subject: History, archaeology, literature and art of Italy and the Roman empire down to 700 AD

350   Omohundro Institute Postdoctoral Fellowship

Awarding body: Omohundro Institute of Early American History and Culture (OIEAHC) (USA)
Address: OIEAHC, PO Box 8781, Williamsburg, VA 23187-8781, USA
Tel: (001) 757 221 1133
Email: ieahc1@wm.edu
Web: http://oieahc.wm.edu/
Contact: Ronald Hoffman, Director
Award: A stipend of US$50,400 to revise the applicant's first book manuscript and the Institute's commitment to publish the resulting study, closing date 1 Nov
Objective: To enable publication of manuscripts which have significant potential as distinguished, book-length contributions to scholarship
Subject: History and cultures of North America from c.1450 to 1820, including related developments in the Caribbean, Latin America, Europe and Africa – in short, any subject encompassing the Atlantic world in this period

351   The Royal Society of Literature Jerwood Awards

Awarding body: Royal Society of Literature
Address: The Royal Society of Literature, Somerset House, Strand, London WC2R 1LA
Tel: 020 7845 4676
Email: paulaj@rslit.org
Web: www.rslit.org/rsl-jerwood-prize/
Contact: Paula Johnson
Award: Three annual awards, one of £10,000 and two of £5,000, to authors engaged on their first major commissioned works of non-fiction
Objective: To provide assistance to authors while they research and write their books
Subject: Any

352 Scholarly Edition Grants

Awarding body: National Endowment for the Humanities (NEH) (USA)
Address: NEH, Division of Research Programs, 1100 Pennsylvania Ave, NW, Room 318, Washington, DC 20506, USA
Email: editions@neh.gov
Web: www.neh.gov/grants/guidelines/editions.html
Award: US$50,000–US$100,000 per year for 1 to 3 years to support the preparation for publication of pre-existing texts and documents that are currently inaccessible or available in inadequate editions, the funding may consist of outright funds, federal matching funds, or a combination of the two, applicants must be US citizens or US residents, or applying through a US-based institution, closing date 5 Dec
Objective: To support a team of at least one editor and one other staff member preparing existing texts for publication so that scholars, educators, students and the public have ready and easy access to these materials
Subject: Humanities projects involving significant literary, philosophical and historical materials are typical in this grant programme, but other types of work, such as musical notation, are also eligible

353 Scouloudi Historical Awards

Awarding body: Institute of Historical Research (IHR) – University of London
Address: IHR, University of London, Senate House, Malet St, London WC1E 7HU
Tel: 020 7862 8740
Fax: 020 7862 8745
Email: james.lees@sas.ac.uk
Web: www.history.ac.uk
Contact: Fellowships Officer
Award: Subsidy towards the cost of publishing a scholarly book or article, or an issue of a learned journal in the field of history, not including expenses incurred in the preparation of a thesis for a higher degree, closing date late Mar
Objective: To pay for research, and other expenses, to be incurred in the completion of advanced historical work, which the applicant intends subsequently to publish
Subject: History

354 Sheldon Memorial Trust Publications Grants

Awarding body: Sheldon Memorial Trust
Address: Sheldon Memorial Trust, 21 School Lane, Copmanthorpe, York YO23 3SQ
Tel: 01904 705530
Web: www.sheldonmemorialtrust.org.uk
Contact: Honorary Secretary
Award: Value £250–£1,000, to aid the publication of material where publication would not be achieved without financial assistance, where a profit is likely the Trust would normally make an interest-free loan
Objective: To assist the publication of material within the Trust's objects
Subject: History, literature or the arts in connection with the City of York

10   Research grants

355   All Souls College Visiting Fellowships

Awarding body: All Souls College – University of Oxford
Address: All Souls College, Oxford OX1 4AL
Tel: 01865 2879308
Fax: 01865 279299
Email: humaira.erfan-ahmed@all-souls.ox.ac.uk
Web: www.all-souls.ox.ac.uk
Contact: Fellows' Secretary
Award: Unspecified number, offered annually, consists of study rooms and residential accommodation, tenable at the College for 1–3 terms non-renewable, closing date 6 Sept
Objective: To encourage personal study and research with the opportunity of lecturing and participation in seminars, for established scholars within normal retiring age
Subject: All subjects

356   American Association for the History of Nursing Grants for Historical Research

Awarding body: American Association for the History of Nursing (AAHN) (USA)
Address: AAHN, 10200 W 44th Ave, #304, Wheat Ridge, CO 80033, USA
Tel: (001) 303 422 2685
Fax: (001) 303 422 8894
Email: aahn@aahn.org
Web: www.aahn.org/grants.html
Award: Value US$2,000 for graduate students, US$3,000 for new researchers (holding a doctorate), applicants must be members of AAHN, closing date 1 Apr

Objective: To ensure the growth of scholarly work focused on the history of nursing
Subject: History of nursing

357   Anderson Fund

Awarding body: Society for Nautical Research
Address: Society for Nautical Research, The Lodge, The Drive, Hellingly, East Sussex BN237 4EP
Email: research@snr.org.uk
Web: www.snr.org.uk/pages/research/anderson-fund
Contact: Dr Edward Hampshire, Secretary of the Research, Technical and Programme Committee
Award: Grants of up to £2,000 to support research into any aspect of maritime history
Objective: To support research
Subject: Maritime history

358 Arts and Humanities Research Council Research Programmes – Fellowships Scheme

Awarding body: Arts and Humanities Research Council (AHRC)
Address: AHRC, Polaris House, North Star Ave, Swindon SN2 1FL
Tel: 01793 41 6000
Email: enquiries@ahrc.ac.uk
Web: www.ahrc.ac.uk/Funding-Opportunities/Pages/Fellowships.aspx
Contact: See website
Award: Open to staff at higher education institutions in Britain, value £50,000–£250,000 for 6–18 months, no closing date
Objective: To assist researchers and support teams or projects
Subject: Arts and humanities

359 Arts and Humanities Research Council Research Programmes – Research Grants Scheme

Awarding body: Arts and Humanities Research Council (AHRC)
Address: AHRC, Polaris House, North Star Ave, Swindon SN2 1FL
Tel: 01793 41 6000
Email: enquiries@ahrc.ac.uk
Web: www.ahrc.ac.uk/Funding-Opportunities/Research-funding/Pages/Research-funding.aspx
Contact: See website
Award: Open to staff at HEIs in Britain, value max £1,000,000 for up to 5 years, no closing date
Objective: To assist researchers and support teams and projects
Subject: Arts and humanities

360 Asia Research Institute Research Fellowships

Awarding body: Asia Research Institute – National University of Singapore (Singapore)
Address: Human Resources, Asia Research Institute, National University of Singapore, 469A Tower Block, #10-01 Bukit Timah Road, Singapore 259770
Tel: (0065) 6516 3810
Fax: (0065) 6779 1428
Email: joinari@nus.edu.sg
Web: www.ari.nus.edu.sg/article_view.asp?id=1461
Contact: Ms Verene Koh
Award: Postdoctoral fellowships, (senior) research fellowships and visiting (senior) research fellowships with varying remuneration and benefits packages, help with travel expenses and fieldwork and conference attendance are available for eligible candidates
Objective: To enable outstanding active researchers from around the world to work on an important piece of research
Subject: Various research clusters in the social sciences and humanities

361 Brill Fellowship at CHASE

Awarding body: Warburg Institute – University of London
Address: Warburg Institute, University of London, Woburn Sq, London WC1H 0AB
Tel: 020 7862 8949
Fax: 020 7862 8955
Email: warburg@sas.ac.uk
Web: http://warburg.sas.ac.uk/fellowships/
Contact: Institute Manager

Award: Up to 2 offered, value up to £3,600 for 2–3 months, open to those with at least a year's doctoral research and, if postdoctoral, must normally have been awarded their doctorate within the preceding 5 years, closing date 30 Nov
Objective: To promote research
Subject: Relations between Europe and the Arab World from the middle ages to the 19th century

362   British Academy Mid-Career Fellowships

Awarding body: British Academy
Address: British Academy, 10 Carlton House Terrace, London SW1Y 5AH
Tel: 020 7969 5200
Fax: 020 7969 5300
Email: grants@britac.ac.uk
Web: www.britac.ac.uk
Contact: Research Awards Team
Award: At least 35 awards, to enable established scholars within 15 years of the award of their doctorate to have research time for between 6 and 12 months to prepare work for publication and communicate the results to a wide audience, closing date 18 Sept
Objective: To enable established researchers to undertake or complete research, aimed at mid-career staff
Subject: Humanities and social sciences

363   British Academy Senior Research Fellowships

Awarding body: British Academy
Address: British Academy, 10 Carlton House Terrace, London SW1Y 5AH
Tel: 020 7969 5200
Fax: 020 7969 5300
Email: posts@britac.ac.uk
Web: www.britac.ac.uk
Contact: Research Awards Team
Award: Senior research fellowships

enabling research leave for 1 year, 7 awards, closing date 20 Nov
Objective: To enable established researchers to undertake or complete research
Subject: Humanities and social sciences

364   British Academy Small Research Grants

Awarding body: British Academy
Address: British Academy, 10 Carlton House Terrace, London SW1Y 5AH
Tel: 020 7969 5200
Fax: 020 7969 5300
Email: grants@britac.ac.uk
Web: www.britac.ac.uk
Contact: Research Awards Team
Award: Value max £10,000, postdoctoral, closing dates 16 Oct, 15 Apr
Objective: To support primary research for collaborative or individual research projects
Subject: Humanities and social sciences

365 British Institute at Ankara Study Grants

Awarding body: British Institute at Ankara (BIAA)
Address: BIAA, 10 Carlton House Terrace, London SW1Y 5AH
Tel: 020 7969 5204
Fax: 020 7969 5401
Email: biaa@britac.ac.uk
Web: www.biaa.ac.uk
Contact: Claire McCafferty
Award: Value up to £2,000, open to doctoral or postdoctoral researchers based at UK institutions, see website for deadlines
Objective: To support scholars in defined aspects of doctoral research which will significantly progress the research, in the completion of PhDs, or in discrete pieces of postdoctoral research, not intended to support fieldwork
Subject: Arts, humanities and the social sciences relating to Turkey and the Black Sea littoral

366 British Institute in Eastern Africa Minor Grants

Awarding body: British Institute in Eastern Africa (Kenya)
Address: The British Institute in Eastern Africa, Liakipia, Nairobi,
Tel: (00254) 20 434 7195
Fax: (00254) 20 434 3365
Email: grants@biea.ac.uk
Web: www.biea.ac.uk
Contact: Ambreena Manji, Director
Award: Contributions towards actual research costs, up to £1,000, closing date 31 March
Objective: To support original research across the region
Subject: Any field of the humanities and social sciences

367 British School at Athens Knossos Research Fund

Awarding body: British School at Athens (BSA) (Greece)
Address: BSA, 52 Souedias, 10676 Athens, Greece
Tel: (0030) 211 1022 800
Fax: (0030) 211 1022 803
Email: school.administrator@bsa.ac.uk
Web: www.bsa.ac.uk
Contact: School Administrator
Award: Variable amounts to support specific projects related to Knossos
Objective: To promote research into, and knowledge of, Knossos in all aspects and across all periods through supporting specific projects and contributing to the infrastructure at Knossos for research
Subject: History of Knossos

368 Browning Fund

Awarding body: British Academy
Address: British Academy, 10 Carlton House Terrace, London SW1Y 5AH
Tel: 020 7969 5200
Fax: 020 7969 5300
Email: grants@britac.ac.uk
Web: www.britac.ac.uk
Contact: Research Awards Team
Award: Variable number, grants up to total value of £10,000, apply through British Academy Small Research Grants scheme, closing date 16 Oct
Objective: To support original research in the field of British history in the early modern period, with particular reference to the 17th century
Subject: Early modern British history

369 BSHS Research Grants

Awarding body: British Society for the History of Science (BSHS)
Address: BSHS Executive Secretary, PO Box 3401, Norwich NR7 7JF
Email: office@bshs.org.uk
Web: http://bshs.org.uk/grants/research-grants/
Contact: Executive Secretary
Award: Small grants of £50–£500 for specific research purposes, such as archival visits, research trips, photography or microfilming, or temporary research assistance costs, open to doctoral and postdoctoral scholars, closing dates 30 Sept, 31 Mar
Objective: To support research
Subject: History of science, technology or medicine

370 Carnegie Collaborative Larger Grants

Awarding body: Carnegie Trust for the Universities of Scotland
Address: Carnegie Trust for the Universities of Scotland, Andrew Carnegie House, Pittencrieff St, Dunfermline KY12 8AW
Tel: 01383 724990
Fax: 01383 749799
Email: pkrus@carnegie-trust.org
Web: www.carnegie-trust.org
Contact: Secretary and Treasurer
Award: Up to £40,000 per project, deadline 1 Feb
Objective: Open to established members of staff of Scottish universities wishing to develop a collaborative research project with other Scottish academics, through the establishment of a network, organisation of explorative seminars, development of new methodologies or testing of new ideas
Subject: Any subject

371 Carnegie Small Research Grants

Awarding body: Carnegie Trust for the Universities of Scotland
Address: Carnegie Trust for the Universities of Scotland, Andrew Carnegie House, Pittencrieff St, Dunfermline KY12 8AW
Tel: 01383 724990
Fax: 01383 749799
Email: pkrus@carnegie-trust.org
Web: www.carnegie-trust.org
Contact: Secretary and Treasurer
Award: A variable number offered throughout the year, value up to £2,200, closing dates 15 Oct, 15 Jan, 15 May, except for research grants of £1,000 and under, which can be considered at any time
Objective: To support established members of staff of Scottish universities in undertaking personal research projects or publication of books
Subject: Any subject

372 Chemical Heritage Foundation Fellowships

Awarding body: Chemical Heritage Foundation (CHF) (USA)
Address: CHF, 315 Chestnut St, Philadelphia, PA 19106-2702, USA
Tel: (001) 215 873 8289
Email: fellowships@chemheritage.org
Web: www.chemheritage.org
Contact: Fellowship Co-ordinator
Award: Various fellowships and scholarships available, see website for details
Objective: For specific projects as advertised
Subject: History of science, the history of chemistry and the chemical process

373 Collaborative Research Grants

Awarding body: National Endowment for the Humanities (NEH) (USA)
Address: NEH, Office of Public Affairs, 1100 Pennsylvania Ave, NW, Washington, DC 20506, USA
Tel: (001) 202 606 8200
Email: info@neh.gov
Web: www.neh.gov/grants/guidelines/collaborative.html
Contact: Lydia Medici
Award: Value US$25,000–$100,000 pa for up to 3 years to support research on a topic in the humanities, funding may consist of outright funds, federal matching funds, or a combination of the two, applicants must be US citizens or residents, or applying through a US-based institution, closing date 5 Dec
Objective: Grants support original research undertaken by a team of 2 or more scholars, or research co-ordinated by an individual scholar that, because of its scope or complexity, requires additional staff and resources beyond the individual's salary
Subject: Humanities subjects

374 Council for British Research in the Levant Pilot Study Awards

Awarding body: Council for British Research in the Levant
Address: Council for British Research in the Levant, c/o British Academy, 10 Carlton House Terrace, London SW1Y 5AH
Tel: 020 7969 5296
Fax: 020 7969 5401
Email: cbrl@britac.ac.uk
Web: www.cbrl.org.uk
Award: Number varies, offered annually, value up to £7,500, closing date 1 Dec

Objective: To support initial exploratory work for research projects in the countries of the Levant as a prelimary to making applications for major funding, projects must include an element of travel to (or from) one of the countries of the Levant
Subject: Humanities and social science subjects including archaeology and historical studies relating to countries of the Levant

375 Dan David Prize Scholarships

Awarding body: Dan David Prize/Tel Aviv University (Israel)
Address: The Dan David Prize, Eitan Bergas Bldg/119, Tel-Aviv University, PO Box 39040, Ramat Aviv, Tel-Aviv 69978, Israel
Tel: (00972) 3 6406614
Fax: (00972) 3 6406613
Email: ddprize@post.tau.ac.il
Web: www.dandavidprize.org
Contact: Ms Smadar Fisher, Director
Award: Twenty scholarships of US$15,000 awarded each year to outstanding doctoral and postdoctoral students from universities around the world, closing date 28 Feb
Objective: To support research
Subject: Fields chosen annually under themes covering each of past, present and future. For 2014 the fields are 'History & memory'; 'Combating memory loss'; and 'Artificial intelligence'

376 Alan Deyermond Fellowship

Awarding body: Warburg Institute – University of London
Address: Warburg Institute, University of London, Woburn Sq, London WC1H 0AB
Tel: 020 7862 8949

Fax: 020 7862 8955
Email: warburg@sas.ac.uk
Web: http://warburg.sas.ac.uk/fellowships/
Contact: Institute Manager
Award: One offered, value up to £2,500 for 2 months, open to doctoral students and recent PhDs
Objective: To promote research
Subject: Spanish literature, culture or visual arts before 1600 (with a preference for the medieval period)

377   Dover Fund
Awarding body: Hellenic Society
Address: Society for the Promotion of Hellenic Studies, Senate House, Malet St, London WC1E 7HU
Tel: 020 7862 8730
Fax: 020 7862 8731
Email: office@hellenicsociety.org.uk
Web: www.hellenicsociety.org.uk
Contact: Secretary
Award: Variable number and value (usually £50–£400), offered annually, open to students and young researchers, closing date 1 May
Objective: To further study of the history of the Greek language in any period from the bronze age to the 15th century AD, and edition and exegesis of Greek texts
Subject: The history of the Greek language and papyri

378   Economic and Social Research Council Research Grants Scheme
Awarding body: Economic and Social Research Council (ESRC)
Address: Policy and Resources Directorate, ESRC, Polaris House, North Star Ave, Swindon SN2 1UJ
Tel: 01793 413000
Fax: 01793 413001
Web: www.esrc.ac.uk

Award: Various awards, value between £200,000 and £2,000,000, proposals invited at any time
Objective: For research
Subject: Social sciences, including economic and social history

379   Economic History Society Small Research Grants Scheme
Awarding body: Economic History Society
Address: Economic History Society, Department of Economic and Social History, University of Glasgow, Lilybank House, Bute Gardens, Glasgow G12 8QQ
Tel: 0141 330 4662
Fax: 0141 330 4889
Email: ehsocsec@arts.gla.ac.uk
Web: www.ehs.org.uk
Contact: Administrative Secretary
Award: Value up to £5,000, to support the direct costs of research aimed at publication and/or for pilot projects that will form the foundation for applications to other bodies for more substantial funding, closing dates 1 Nov, 1 May
Objective: To encourage small-scale research initiatives or pilot studies
Subject: Economic and social history

380 Émilie Du Châtelet Award for Independent Scholarship

Awarding body: American Society for 18th-Century Studies (ASECS) (USA)
Address: ASECS, PO Box 7867, Wake Forest University, Winston-Salem, NC 27109, USA
Tel: (001) 336 727 4694
Fax: (001) 336 727 4697
Email: asecs@wfu.edu
Web: http://asecs.press.jhu.edu/
Contact: Émilie Du Châtelet Award
Award: Awarded by the women's caucus of ASECS, value US$500, open to those with the PhD but who do not hold a position that supports research, closing date 15 Jan
Objective: To support research by an independent scholar
Subject: Feminist or women's studies in an 18th-century cultural context

381 Frances A Yates Research Fellowships (Long-Term)

Awarding body: Warburg Institute – University of London
Address: Warburg Institute, University of London, Woburn Sq, London WC1H 0AB
Tel: 020 7862 8949
Fax: 020 7862 8955
Email: warburg@sas.ac.uk
Web: http://warburg.sas.ac.uk/fellowships/
Contact: Institute Manager
Award: One fellowship of 2 or 3 years, value £27,385 pa, open to those with at least a year's doctoral research and, if postdoctoral, must normally have been awarded their doctorate within the preceding 5 years, closing date 30 Nov
Objective: To promote research

Subject: Cultural and intellectual history, especially of the medieval and Renaissance periods

382 Frances A Yates Research Fellowships

Awarding body: Warburg Institute – University of London
Address: Warburg Institute, University of London, Woburn Sq, London WC1H 0AB
Tel: 020 7862 8949
Fax: 020 7862 8955
Email: warburg@sas.ac.uk
Web: http://warburg.sas.ac.uk/fellowships/
Contact: Institute Manager
Award: A number of 2-, 3- and 4-month fellowships available, value up to £4,800, open to those with at least 1 year's doctoral research or, if postdoctoral, must normally have been awarded their doctorate within the preceding 5 years, closing date 30 Nov
Objective: To promote research
Subject: Cultural and intellectual history, especially of the medieval and Renaissance periods

383 Fritz Thyssen Stiftung Support

Awarding body: Fritz Thyssen Stiftung für Wissenschaftsförderung (Germany)
Address: Fritz Thyssen Stiftung, Am Römerturm 3, D-50667 Köln, Germany
Tel: (0049) 221 27 74 960
Fax: (0049) 221 27 74 96 196
Email: fts@Fritz-Thyssen-Stiftung.de
Web: www.Fritz-Thyssen-Stiftung.de
Award: Awards to cover salaries and research expenses, closing dates end Jan, end Sept

Objective: To support scholarship and research in universities and non-profit research institutions, primarily in Germany, with special emphasis on giving help to young scholars and scientists
Subject: Humanities and international relations

384 Gerald Averay Wainwright Near Eastern Archaeological Fund

Awarding body: Oriental Institute – University of Oxford
Address: Gerald Averay Wainwright Near Eastern Archaeological Fund, Oriental Institute, Pusey Lane, Oxford OX1 2LE
Email: wainwright.fund@orinst.ox.ac.uk
Web: www.wainwrightfund.org.uk
Award: Closing dates 1 Oct, 1 Apr
Objective: To support individual research, particularly by scholars without other regular sources of income, on the study of non-classical archaeology and history as deduced from comparative archaeology in the Near East
Subject: Non-classical archaeology and history as deduced from comparative archaeology in the Near East

385 The Gladys Krieble Delmas Foundation Grants for Independent Research on Venetian History and Culture

Awarding body: Gladys Krieble Delmas Foundation (USA)
Address: The Gladys Krieble Delmas Foundation, 275 Madison Ave, 33rd Floor, New York, NY 10016-1101, USA
Tel: (001) 212 687 0011
Fax: (001) 212 687 8877
Email: info@delmas.org
Web: www.delmas.org

Contact: Rachel Kimber
Award: Grants of up to US$19,900 available for travel to and residence in Venice and the Veneto, closing date 15 Dec
Objective: To support historical research on Venice and the former Venetian empire and the study of contemporary Venice
Subject: Disciplines of the humanities and social sciences are eligible areas of study

386 Grete Sondheimer Fellowship

Awarding body: Warburg Institute – University of London
Address: Warburg Institute, University of London, Woburn Sq, London WC1H 0AB
Tel: 020 7862 8949
Fax: 020 7862 8955
Email: warburg@sas.ac.uk
Web: http://warburg.sas.ac.uk/fellowships/
Contact: Institute Manager
Award: One offered, value up to £2,500 for 2 months, open to those with at least 1 year's doctoral research or, if postdoctoral, must normally have been awarded their doctorate within the preceding 5 years, closing date 30 Nov
Objective: To promote research
Subject: Cultural and intellectual history, especially of the medieval and Renaissance periods

387   Hayek Fund for Scholars

Awarding body: Institute for Humane Studies (IHS) – George Mason University (USA)
Address: IHS, George Mason University, 3351 Fairfax Dr, MSN 1C5, Arlington, VA 22201-4432, USA
Tel: (001) 703 993 4880
Fax: (001) 703 993 4890
Email: hayekfund@ihs.gmu.edu
Web: www.theihs.org
Award: Value up to US$750
Objective: To support graduate students and untenured faculty members in career-enhancing activities
Subject: Subjects connected with humane studies and the study of liberty

388   Henri Frankfort Research Fellowship

Awarding body: Warburg Institute – University of London
Address: Warburg Institute, University of London, Woburn Sq, London WC1H 0AB
Tel: 020 7862 8949
Fax: 020 7862 8955
Email: warburg@sas.ac.uk
Web: http://warburg.sas.ac.uk/fellowships/
Contact: Institute Manager
Award: One offered, value up to £3,600 for 2–3 months, open to those with at least 1 year's doctoral research or, if postdoctoral, must normally have been awarded their doctorate within the preceding 5 years, closing date 30 Nov
Objective: To promote research in the intellectual and cultural history of the ancient Near East, not intended to support archaeological excavation
Subject: The intellectual and cultural history of the ancient Near East

389   Historic Society of Lancashire and Cheshire Research Grants

Awarding body: Historic Society of Lancashire and Cheshire
Address: Historic Society of Lancashire and Cheshire, School of History, University of Liverpool, Liverpool L69 3BX
Web: www.hslc.org.uk
Contact: Dr D E Ascott
Award: Grants of up to £300 to cover research expenses, closing date 31 Oct
Objective: Awarded for the study of any aspect of the history and archaeology of Lancashire or Cheshire, to help cover expenses such as travel to an archive or the acquisition of copied resources, applicants should usually be registered for a research degree or have an established publication record
Subject: History of Lancashire and Cheshire

390   Humane Studies Fellowships

Awarding body: Institute for Humane Studies (IHS) – George Mason University (USA)
Address: IHS, George Mason University, 3351 Fairfax Dr, MSN 1C5, Arlington, VA 22201-4432, USA
Tel: (001) 703 993 4880
Fax: (001) 703 993 4890
Email: hsf@ihs.gmu.edu
Web: www.theihs.org
Award: Offered annually, value up to US$15,000, open to graduate and undergraduate students, closing date 31 Dec
Objective: To support outstanding students with a demonstrable interest in the classical liberal tradition

Subject: Subjects connected with humane studies and the study of liberty

391   IEEE Life Members' Fellowship in Electrical History

Awarding body: IEEE (USA)
Address: IEEE History Center, Rutgers, The State University of New Jersey, 39 Union St, New Brunswick, NJ 08901, USA
Tel: (001) 732 562 5450
Fax: (001) 732 932 1193
Email: ieee-history@ieee.org
Web: www.ieee.org/web/aboutus/history_center/about/fellowship.html
Contact: Chair, IEEE Fellowship in Electrical History Committee
Award: One offered annually, stipend US$17,000 for 1 year, plus US$3,000 for research, to cover either 1 year of full-time postgraduate study or 1 year of postdoctoral research, closing date 1 Feb
Objective: To support graduate research
Subject: History of electrical engineering and technology

392   Institute of Classical Studies Visiting Fellowships

Awarding body: Institute of Classical Studies – University of London
Address: Institute of Classical Studies, Senate House, Malet St, London WC1E 7HU
Tel: 020 7862 8700
Fax: 020 7862 8722
Email: admin.icls@sas.ac.uk
Web: www.icls.sas.ac.uk
Contact: Secretary
Award: Open to classical scholars from the UK and abroad, tenable for 3–12 months
Objective: To support study
Subject: Classical studies

393   Jacobite Studies Trust Fellowships in History

Awarding body: Institute of Historical Research (IHR) – University of London
Address: IHR, University of London, Senate House, Malet St, London WC1E 7HU
Tel: 020 7862 8740
Email: james.lees@sas.ac.uk
Web: www.history.ac.uk
Contact: James Lees
Award: Two 6-month non-residential fellowships, stipend of £7,500, open to current doctoral students who have been registered on their programme for at least 3 years full-time (6 years part-time) and those who have received a PhD within the last two years, closing date 1 Feb
Objective: To support historical research into the Stuart dynasty in the British Isles and in exile, from the departure of James II in 1688 to the death of Henry Benedict Stuart in 1807
Subject: The Stuart dynasty, including their supporters, activities, influence, ideologies, political and cultural context, and other related topics

394   Janet Arnold Award

Awarding body: Society of Antiquaries of London
Address: Society of Antiquaries of London, Burlington House, Piccadilly, London W1J 0BE
Tel: 020 7479 7080
Fax: 020 7287 6987
Email: hcockle@sal.org.uk
Web: www.sal.org.uk/grants/janetarnold/
Contact: Research Committee
Award: Funding for travel, accommodation and incidental expenses, usual value £350–2,000, closing date 15 Jan
Objective: To encourage original research based on items of Western dress or their remains resulting in publication, display, cataloguing or teaching, or for practical use in conservation or reproduction
Subject: History of Western dress

395   John Morrison Memorial Fund for Hellenic Maritime Studies

Awarding body: British School at Athens (BSA) (Greece)
Address: BSA, 52 Souedias, 106 76 Athens, Greece
Tel: (0030) 211 1022 800
Fax: (0030) 211 1022 803
Email: assistant.director@bsa.ac.uk
Web: www.bsa.ac.uk
Contact: Assistant Director
Award: Grant of up to £500 for research expenses, closing date 1 Apr
Objective: To further research into all branches of Hellenic maritime studies of any period
Subject: Hellenic maritime studies of any period

396   Larry J Hackman Research Residency Program

Awarding body: New York State Archives (USA)
Address: NYS Archives Partnership Trust, Cultural Education Center, Suite 9C49, Albany, NY 12230, USA
Tel: (001) 518 473 7091
Fax: (001) 518-473-7058
Email: hackmanres@mail.nysed.gov
Web: www.nysarchivestrust.org
Contact: Dr James D Folts, Head, Research Services
Award: Value US$100–US$4,500, open to those undertaking doctoral dissertations or those at postdoctoral level, closing date 15 Jan
Objective: To support advanced research
Subject: New York history, government or public policy

397   Leverhulme Research Fellowships

Awarding body: Leverhulme Trust
Address: Research Awards Advisory Committee, Leverhulme Trust, 1 Pemberton Row, London EC4A 3BG
Tel: 020 7042 9861
Fax: 020 7042 9889
Email: agrundy@leverhulme.ac.uk
Web: www.leverhulme.ac.uk
Contact: Anna Grundy
Award: Approx 95 offered, value max £45,000, for 3–24 months, open to experienced researchers prevented by routine duties from undertaking/completing research, closing date 7 Nov
Objective: To provide a period devoted to full-time research, for replacement teaching costs, loss of earnings and/or research expenses
Subject: All subjects

398   Leverhulme Trust Emeritus Fellowships

Awarding body: Leverhulme Trust
Address: Research Awards Advisory Committee, Leverhulme Trust, 1 Pemberton Row, London EC4A 3BG
Tel: 020 7042 9861
Fax: 020 7042 9889
Email: agrundy@leverhulme.ac.uk
Web: www.leverhulme.ac.uk
Contact: Anna Grundy
Award: Approx 35 offered annually, value according to individual assessment up to £22,000, tenable in the UK or abroad for between 3 months and 2 years, closing date 6 Feb
Objective: To assist experienced researchers in completion of research already begun, open to those who will have retired by the time they take up the award and who have held full-time teaching/research posts in the UK
Subject: Any subject

399   Leverhulme Trust International Academic Fellowships

Awarding body: Leverhulme Trust
Address: Research Awards Advisory Committee, Leverhulme Trust, 1 Pemberton Row, London EC4A 3BG
Tel: 020 7042 9862
Fax: 020 7042 9889
Email: bkerr@leverhulme.ac.uk
Web: www.leverhulme.ac.uk
Contact: Bridget Kerr
Award: Approx 10 offered, max value £30,000, for 3–12 months for a concentrated period overseas, for replacement costs, travel and subsistence and essential support costs (e.g. laboratory or office consumables), closing date 7 Nov
Objective: To enable established academics to devote time overseas to the exchange of ideas, the development of new collaborations, developing innovations in teaching, or the opportunity for 'discipline-hopping excursions' into new areas of research.
Subject: All subjects

400   Leverhulme Trust International Networks

Awarding body: Leverhulme Trust
Address: Research Awards Advisory Committee, Leverhulme Trust, 1 Pemberton Row, London EC4A 3BG
Tel: 020 7042 9873
Fax: 020 7042 9889
Email: nthorp@leverhulme.ac.uk
Contact: Matt Dillnutt
Award: Max value £125,000 for up to 3 years of activity, refer to the Trust's website for full details of eligible costs within this scheme
Objective: To enable a Principal Investigator based in the UK to lead a research project where its successful completion is dependent on the participation of relevant overseas institutions
Subject: All subjects

401 Leverhulme Trust Major Research Fellowships

Awarding body: Leverhulme Trust
Address: Research Awards Advisory Committee, Leverhulme Trust, 1 Pemberton Row, London EC4A 3BG
Tel: 020 7042 9872
Fax: 020 7042 9889
Email: nthorp@leverhulme.ac.uk
Web: www.leverhulme.ac.uk
Contact: Nicola Thorp
Award: Approx 30 offered, support for replacement costs and up to £5,000 pa for research expenses provided for fellowships of 2 or 3 years, closing date May
Objective: To enable well-established and distinguished researchers in the humanities and social sciences to devote themselves to a single research project of outstanding originality and significance
Subject: Humanities and social sciences

402 Leverhulme Trust Research Project Grants

Awarding body: Leverhulme Trust
Address: Research Awards Advisory Committee, Leverhulme Trust, 1 Pemberton Row, London EC4A 3BG
Tel: 020 7042 9873
Fax: 020 7042 9889
Email: mdillnutt@leverhulme.ac.uk
Web: www.leverhulme.ac.uk
Contact: Matt Dillnutt
Award: Variable number offered, value usually up to £250,000 for a period of 2–3 years, the grants provide support for the salaries of research staff engaged on the project, plus associated costs directly related to the research proposed
Objective: For innovative and original research projects of high quality and potential, the choice of theme and the

design of the research lying entirely with the applicant
Subject: Any subject

403 Macmillan-Rodewald Studentship

Awarding body: British School at Athens (BSA) (Greece)
Address: BSA, 52 Souedias, 106 76 Athens, Greece
Tel: (0030) 211 1022 800
Fax: (0030) 211 1022 803
Email: school.administrator@bsa.ac.uk
Web: www.bsa.ac.uk
Contact: Tania Gerousi
Award: Value AHRC's London-based rate for postgraduate awards, 1 year renewable, closing date 15 Apr
Objective: For advanced doctoral or postdoctoral research in Greece, candidates are expected to have completed at least 1 year's doctoral research
Subject: Any aspect of the history and archaeology of Greece

404 Mark Samuels Lasner Fellowship in Printing History

Awarding body: American Printing History Association (APHA) (USA)
Address: American Printing History Association, PO Box 4519, Grand Central Station, New York, NY 10163-4519, USA
Email: sgcrook@printinghistory.org
Web: www.printinghistory.org/programs/fellowship-program.php
Contact: Executive Secretary
Award: Award of up to US$2,000 towards travel, living and other research expenses, closing date 2 Dec
Objective: To support research

Subject: Any area of the history of printing in all its forms, including all the arts and technologies relevant to printing, the book arts and letter forms

405   Michael Ventris Memorial Award

Awarding body: Institute of Classical Studies – University of London
Address: Institute of Classical Studies, Senate House, Malet St, London WC1E 7HU
Tel: 020 7862 8700
Fax: 020 7862 8722
Email: admin.icls@sas.ac.uk
Web: www.icls.sas.ac.uk
Contact: Secretary
Award: One offered annually, value £2,000, for young scholars who have received the doctorate in the last 8 years, closing date 15 Jan
Objective: To promote the study of the Mycenaean civilisation
Subject: Mycenaean studies

406   NASA Fellowship in Aerospace History

Awarding body: American Historical Association (AHA) (USA)
Address: AHA, 400 A St, SE Washington, DC 20003, USA
Tel: (001) 202 544 2422
Fax: (001) 202 544 8307
Email: awards@historians.org
Web: www.historians.org/prizes/
Contact: Administrative Office Assistant
Award: Value US$20,000 for 6–9 months, open to PhD students and beyond, closing date 1 Apr
Objective: To support research
Subject: Aerospace history

407   National Endowment for the Humanities Fellowships/Faculty Research Awards

Awarding body: National Endowment for the Humanities (NEH) (USA)
Address: NEH, Division of Research Programs, 1100 Pennsylvania Ave, NW, Room 318, Washington, DC 20506, USA
Tel: (001) 202 606 8200
Email: fellowships@neh.gov
Web: www.neh.gov/grants/guidelines/fellowships.html
Award: Value US$4,200 per month for 6–12 months, fellowships open to US citizens or residents, faculty research awards open for faculty members at historically black, Hispanic-serving and tribal colleges and universities, closing date 31 May
Objective: To support individuals pursuing advanced research in the humanities that contributes to scholarly knowledge or to the general public's understanding of the humanities
Subject: Humanities

408   New Zealand History Research Trust Fund Awards

Awarding body: New Zealand – Ministry for Culture and Heritage (New Zealand)
Address: History Group, Ministry for Culture and Heritage, PO Box 5364, Wellington, New Zealand
Tel: (0064) 4 499 4229
Fax: (0064) 4 499 4490
Email: historyaward@mch.govt.nz
Web: www.mch.govt.nz/awards/
Contact: Tim Shoebridge
Award: One award of NZ$60,000 offered annually, with other awards of up to NZ$12,000 (up to a total of NZ$120,000–NZ$150,000 available annually), closing date 15 Oct
Objective: To support reseachers and writers of projects relating to New Zealand history, to enable research in New Zealand or abroad
Subject: New Zealand history

409   New Zealand Oral History Awards

Awarding body: New Zealand – Ministry for Culture and Heritage
Address: History Group, Ministry for Culture and Heritage, PO Box 5364, Wellington, New Zealand
Tel: (0064) 4 499 4229
Fax: (0064) 4 499 4490
Email: alison.parr@mch.govt.nz
Web: www.mch.govt.nz/awards/
Contact: Alison Parr
Award: Up to about NZ$100,000 available annually, closing date 30 Apr
Objective: To support the recording of oral history projects
Subject: New Zealand history

410   Nuffield College Postdoctoral Prize Research Fellowships

Awarding body: Nuffield College – University of Oxford

Address: PPRF Competition, Nuffield College, New Rd, Oxford OX1 1NF
Tel: 01865 278516
Fax: 01865 278621
Email: pprf@nuffield.ox.ac.uk
Web: www.nuffield.ox.ac.uk
Contact: Administrative Officer
Award: Value in 2013–14 £23,315 plus accommodation or £5,340 pa housing grant, open to PhD students or recent doctorates, up to 4 awarded annually, closing date early Nov
Objective: To support research
Subject: Social sciences, including recent history and international relations

411   Phillips Fund Grants for Native American Research

Awarding body: American Philosophical Society (USA)
Address: Phillips Fund Grants, American Philosophical Society, 104 S 5th St, Philadelphia, PA 19106-3387, USA
Tel: (001) 215 440 3429
Email: lmusumeci@amphilsoc.org
Web: www.amphilsoc.org/grants/phillips/
Contact: Linda Musumeci, director of grants and fellowships
Award: Value up to US$3,500, for 1 year, open to younger postdoctoral scholars or those researching the Master's or PhD, closing date 3 Mar
Objective: To support extra costs of research, such as travel, tapes, films and consultants' fees
Subject: Native American linguistics, ethnohistory and the history of studies of Native Americans, in the US and Canada

412 Richard Bradford McConnell Fund for Landscape Studies

Awarding body: British School at Athens (BSA) (Greece)
Address: BSA, 52 Souedias, 106 76 Athens, Greece
Tel: (0030) 211 1022 800
Fax: (0030) 211 1022 803
Email: school.administrator@bsa.ac.uk
Web: www.bsa.ac.uk
Contact: School Administrator
Award: Value up to £400 to cover research expenses, closing date 1 Apr
Objective: To support research into the interaction between place and people in Greece and Cyprus at any period
Subject: Arts, humanities and social sciences

413 Robert and Lisa Sainsbury Fellowships

Awarding body: British Association for Japanese Studies (BAJS)
Address: BAJS, University of Essex, Wivenhoe Park, Colchester CO4 3SQ
Tel: 01206 872543
Fax: 01206 873965
Email: bajs@bajs.org.uk
Web: www.bajs.org.uk
Contact: BAJS Secretariat
Award: One award of £23,500 for 1 year and 2 or 3 awards of £8,000–£12,000 for 3–6 months, office space at the Sainsbury Institute, open to scholars who either hold a PhD from a North American, European or Asian university or who are currently affiliated with an academic institution or museum, closing date 1 Mar
Objective: To support research
Subject: Any area of Japanese culture, with preference for history of art, cultural heritage, archaeology or architecture

414 Royal Society Research Grants

Awarding body: Royal Society
Address: Royal Society, 6–9 Carlton House Terrace, London SW1Y 5AG
Tel: 020 7451 2539
Fax: 020 7451 2543
Email: ukgrants@royalsociety.org
Web: http://royalsociety.org/grants/
Contact: Grants Team
Award: Number varies, value up to £5,000 to aid publication of scholarly works in the history of science or up to £15,000 to support research in the history of science, open to untenured researchers and retired scientists resident in the UK as well as tenured scientists
Objective: To provide support for research in the history of science and to assist with the publication of scholarly works in the history of science
Subject: History of science

415 Sino-British Fellowship Trust

Awarding body: British Academy
Address: British Academy, 10 Carlton House Terrace, London SW1Y 5AH
Tel: 020 7969 5200
Fax: 020 7969 5300
Email: grants@britac.ac.uk
Web: www.britac.ac.uk
Contact: Research Awards Team
Award: Variable number, grants up to total value of £10,000, apply through British Academy Small Research Grants scheme, closing date 16 Oct
Objective: To support individual or co-operative research projects, involving Chinese scholars or scholars of Chinese origin, conducted in China, and involving person-to-person contacts
Subject: Humanities and social sciences

416   Sir John Plumb Charitable Trust

Awarding body: Sir John Plumb Charitable Trust
Address: Gonville and Caius College, Cambridge CB2 1TA
Tel: 01223 332454
Fax: 01223 332456
Email: jw10005@cam.ac.uk
Web: www.hist.cam.ac.uk
Contact: Professor Joachim Whaley
Award: Awards of up to £500, open to undergraduate and postgraduate students, including those not at the University, closing date 24 Jan
Objective: For research, the publication of that research and the writing of history
Subject: History

417   Society of Antiquaries of London Research Grants

Awarding body: Society of Antiquaries of London
Address: Society of Antiquaries of London, Burlington House, Piccadilly, London W1J 0BE
Tel: 020 7479 7080
Fax: 020 7287 6967
Email: hcockle@sal.org.uk
Web: www.sal.org.uk/grants/minorresearchgrants/
Contact: Research Committee
Award: Value £500–£5,000, open to all, except students, for research in all aspects of the material past, awards may be named in honour of the following benefactors: Hugh Chapman (for research projects on the western Roman Empire and antiquarian matters in London and its environs), Joan Pye (for early-career researchers (within 5 years of completing their PhD), in the fields of prehistoric and Roman archaeology in the UK) or Marion Wilson (research

projects in southern Britain), closing date 15 Jan
Objective: To support projects that entail new initiatives and/or create interdisciplinary interest; projects of definable scale or duration to which the Society will be a significant contributor; projects based on funds derived from a number of sources to which the Society will be one contributor (but not those which simply 'top up' applications to major funding bodies). Although part of a larger project, the Society's grants should be used to support a definable objective with concrete outcomes
Subject: Archaeology and antiquity

418   Society of Antiquaries of Scotland Research Grants

Awarding body: Society of Antiquaries of Scotland
Address: Society of Antiquaries of Scotland, Royal Museum, Chambers St, Edinburgh EH1 1JF
Tel: 0131 248 4133
Fax: 0131 247 4163
Email: grants@socantscot.org
Web: www.socantscot.org
Contact: Research Committee
Award: Grants available towards the costs of all aspects of archaeological or historical research relating to Scotland, max value £2,000, closing date 30 Nov
Objective: To support research by archaeologists, historians and others for projects such as archaeological fieldwork, museum studies and documentary research
Subject: History, archaeology, archaeological fieldwork, museum studies and documentary research

419   Tebbutt Research Fund

Awarding body: Wealden Iron
Research Group (WIRG)
Address: WIRG, 2 West St Farm
Cottages, Maynards Green,
Heathfield, Sussex TN21 0DG
Email: wirghonsec@hotmail.com
Web: www.wealdeniron.org.uk
Contact: Hon Secretary, David Brown
Award: Grants of up to £100, closing
date 31 Mar
Objective: To aid research into the
iron industry of the Weald
Subject: History and archaeology

420   Theodore C Sorensen Fellowship

Awarding body: John F Kennedy
Library Foundation (USA)
Address: John F Kennedy Library,
Columbia Point, Boston, MA 02125,
USA
Tel: (001) 617 514 1600
Email: kennedy.library@nara.gov
Web: www.jfklibrary.org
Contact: Grant and Fellowships Co-
ordinator
Award: One awarded annually, value
max US$3,600, closing date 15 Aug
Objective: To support a scholar in the
production of a substantial work in
the areas of domestic policy, political
journalism, polling, press relations or
a related topic
Subject: Domestic policy, political
journalism, polling, press relations or
a related topic

421   Vronwy Hankey Memorial Fund

Awarding body: British School at
Athens (BSA) (Greece)
Address: BSA, 52 Souedias, 106 76
Athens, Greece
Tel: (0030) 211 1022 800
Fax: (0030) 211 1022 803

Email: school.administrator@bsa.ac.uk
Web: www.bsa.ac.uk
Contact: School Administrator
Award: Value up to £1,000 to cover
research expenses, closing dates 1
Apr
Objective: To support research
in the prehistory of the Aegean
and its connections with the east
Mediterranean
Subject: Prehistory of the Aegean and
Mediterranean

422   Wardrop Fund for Georgian (Transcaucasia) Studies

Awarding body: Oriental Institute –
University of Oxford
Address: Wardrop Scholarship Fund,
Oriental Institute, Pusey Lane, Oxford
OX1 2LE
Web: www.orinst.ox.ac.uk/general/
grants.html
Contact: Trust Funds Administrator
Award: Duration 2 years with
possibility of a third upon application,
for application form contact Trust
Funds Administrator
Objective: To assist study at the
postgraduate level or postdoctoral
research
Subject: Literature, language and
history of Georgia in Transcaucasia

423   The White House Historical Association Research Grants

Awarding body: White House Historical Association (USA)
Address: Research Grants Program, White House Historical Association, PO Box 27624, Washington, DC 20038-7624, USA
Fax: (001) 202 789 0440
Email: edu@whha.org
Web: www.whitehousehistory.org/whha_about/research_travel-grants.html
Award: Grants of up to US$2,000 towards travel and accommodation costs, preference given to those undertaking dissertation research or postdoctoral research with plans for publication, research may be conducted at the National Archives and Records Administration, presidential libraries or Library of Congress, closing date 1 Mar, 1 Sept
Objective: To encourage new scholarship on the history of the White House
Subject: History of the White House

424   Wolfson College Non-Stipendiary Research Fellowships

Awarding body: Wolfson College – University of Oxford
Address: Wolfson College, Oxford OX2 6UD
Tel: 01865 274102
Fax: 01865 274136
Email: sue.hales@wolfson.ox.ac.uk
Web: www.wolfson.ox.ac.uk
Contact: President's PA
Award: Up to 12 research fellowships offered annually (3 years initially, renewable for 4 years), no stipend but weekly allowance for Common Table meals

Objective: To allow advanced study or research at the College, open to either those with limited research experience (who have recently completed or are about to complete a doctorate) or those who are becoming established scholars in their field
Subject: Humanities and social studies

425   Wolfson College Stipendiary Junior Research Fellowship

Awarding body: Wolfson College – University of Oxford
Address: Wolfson College, Oxford OX2 6UD
Tel: 01865 274102
Fax: 01865 274136
Email: sue.hales@wolfson.ox.ac.uk
Web: www.wolfson.ox.ac.uk
Contact: President's PA
Award: Subject to funds being available, 1 offered in given fields triennially, value £16,072 pa, plus accommodation and meals in hall, tenable at Wolfson for 3 years
Objective: For research, open to those with relevant postgraduate research experience, preference will be given to those holding a doctorate
Subject: Given fields in humanities and social studies, to be decided as Fellowships become available

11 Travel grants

426 American Society for 18th-Century Studies Travel Grants

Awarding body: American Society for 18th-Century Studies (ASECS) (USA)
Address: ASECS, PO Box 7867, Wake Forest University, Winston-Salem, NC 27109, USA
Tel: (001) 336 727 4694
Fax: (001) 336 727 4697
Email: asecs@wfu.edu
Web: http://asecs.press.jhu.edu/
Award: Numerous travel grants open to ASECS members, value US$250–US$1,500, closing dates Nov, Jan
Objective: To support travel to conferences and for research
Subject: 18th-century cultural history

427 American Society for 18th-Century Studies Travelling Jam-Pot: Fund for Graduate Students

Awarding body: American Society for 18th-Century Studies (ASECS) (USA)
Address: ASECS, PO Box 7867, Wake Forest University, Winston-Salem, NC 27109, USA
Tel: (001) 336 727 4694
Fax: (001) 336 727 4697
Email: asecs@wfu.edu
Web: http://asecs.press.jhu.edu/
Contact: Byron Wells, Executive Director
Award: Up to 3 awards of travel costs (up to US$300) for graduate students attending the ASECS annual meeting, deadline 1 Nov
Objective: To support travel to the ASECS annual conference
Subject: 18th-century cultural history

428 BAAS Founders' Research Travel Award

Awarding body: British Association for American Studies (BAAS)
Address: American Studies, School of Humanities, Keele University, Keele, Staffs ST5 5BG
Email: awards@baas.ac.uk
Web: www.baas.ac.uk
Contact: Professor Ian Bell (i.f.a.bell@ams.keele.ac.uk)
Award: Up to 5 offered annually, value £750, open to scholars in the UK who need to travel to conduct research, or who have been invited to read papers at a conference on American studies topics, closing date 14 Dec
Objective: To fund travel in the US
Subject: Subject relating to American histories, culture and society

429 British Academy Ancient Persia Fund Grants

Awarding body: British Academy
Address: British Academy, 10 Carlton House Terrace, London SW1Y 5AH
Tel: 020 7969 5200
Fax: 020 7969 5300
Email: grants@britac.ac.uk
Web: www.britac.ac.uk
Contact: Research Awards Team
Award: Value max £500, towards travel costs, tenable for 1 year, apply through British Academy Small Research Grants scheme, closing date 16 Oct
Objective: To encourage and support the postdoctoral study of Iran and central Asia in the pre-Islamic period
Subject: Iranian or central Asian studies in the pre-Islamic period

430   British Academy International Partnerships and Mobility

Awarding body: British Academy
Address: The British Academy, 10 Carlton House Terrace, London SW1Y 5AH
Tel: 020 7969 5200
Fax: 020 7967 5300
Email: overseas@britac.ac.uk
Web: www.britac.ac.uk
Contact: International Department
Award: One-year or 3-year awards of up to £10,000 pa to support the development of research partnerships between UK scholars and scholars in sub-Saharan Africa, Latin America and the Caribbean, the Middle East and North Africa, South Asia, East and South-East Asia
Objective: To enable the development of long-term links between UK and overseas scholars
Subject: Humanities and social sciences

431   British Association for American Studies Postgraduate Short-Term Travel Awards

Awarding body: British Association for American Studies (BAAS)
Address: American Studies, Sussex Centre for Cultural Studies, University of Sussex, Sussex House, Falmer, Brighton BN1 9RH
Email: awards@baas.ac.uk
Web: www.baas.ac.uk
Contact: Dr Sue Currell (sue.currell@ baas.ac.uk)
Award: Several offered annually, max value £750, duration normally up to 12 weeks, open to postgraduate UK-based scholars, preference may be given to BAAS members, closing date 29 Nov

Objective: To fund travel in the US for research purposes
Subject: Subject relating to American histories, culture and society

432   BSHS Butler-Eyles Travel Grants

Awarding body: British Society for the History of Science (BSHS)
Address: BSHS Executive Secretary, PO Box 3401, Norwich NR7 7JF
Email: office@bshs.org.uk
Web: http://bshs.org.uk/grants/
Contact: Executive Secretary
Award: Grants of up to £100, for travel to BSHS conferences, for postgraduate students or independent scholars
Objective: To support attendance at BSHS conferences
Subject: History of science, technology or medicine

433 Colin Matthew Fund – Travel Awards for Historical Research

Awarding body: Colin Matthew Fund Committee
Address: The Bursar's Secretary, St Hugh's College, Oxford OX2 6LE
Email: amanda.moss@st-hughs.ox.ac.uk
Web: www.orinst.ox.ac.uk/general/grants.html
Contact: Amanda Moss
Award: Award of up to £500, open to Junior Members (undergraduate or postgraduate) of Oxford University, closing date Friday of fourth week of Trinity term (late May)
Objective: To support travel for the purposes of research for a thesis on a historical topic
Subject: History

434 Council for British Research in the Levant Travel Grants

Awarding body: Council for British Research in the Levant
Address: Council for British Research in the Levant, c/o British Academy, 10 Carlton House Terrace, London SW1Y 5AH
Tel: 020 7969 5296
Fax: 020 7969 5401
Email: cbrl@britac.ac.uk
Web: www.cbrl.org.uk
Award: Number varies, offered annually, value up to £800, closing date mid Jan
Objective: To cover costs of travel and subsistence of students, academics and researchers undertaking reconnaissance tours or smaller research projects in the countries of the Levant
Subject: Humanities and social science subjects, including archaeology and historical studies, relating to the countries of the Levant

435 Gunning Jubilee Gift

Awarding body: Society of Antiquaries of Scotland
Address: Society of Antiquaries of Scotland, Royal Museum, Chambers St, Edinburgh EH1 1JF
Tel: 0131 248 4133
Fax: 0131 247 4163
Email: grants@socantscot.org
Web: www.socantscot.org
Contact: Research Committee
Award: Awarded in line with the resources available in any one year, closing date 30 Nov
Objective: To help experts to visit museums, collections or materials of archaeological science, at home or abroad, for the purposes of special investigation and research
Subject: Archaeological or historical research relating to Scotland

436   John J Pisano Travel Grants

Awarding body: National Institutes of Health (USA)
Address: John J Pisano Travel Grants, Building 60, Room 262, National Institutes of Health, Bethesda, MD 20814-1460, USA
Tel: (001) 301 496 6610
Fax: (001) 301 402 1434
Email: history@nih.gov
Web: http://history.nih.gov/research/pisano.html
Contact: David Cantor, Acting Director, Office of History
Award: One or 2 grants of US$1,500 for US residents and US$2,000 for recipients who reside outside the US to travel to the National Institutes of Health
Objective: To encourage historical research relating to the NIH intramural programmes
Subject: History of biomedical sciences and technology

437   Sir Ernest Cassel Educational Trust Fund Grants

Awarding body: British Academy
Address: British Academy, 10 Carlton House Terrace, London SW1Y 5AH
Tel: 020 7969 5200
Fax: 020 7969 5300
Email: grants@britac.ac.uk
Web: www.britac.ac.uk
Contact: Research Awards Team
Award: Variable number offered, value £200–£1,000, apply through British Academy Small Research Grants Scheme for total value of award up to £10,000, closing date 16 Oct
Objective: To assist with overseas travel expenses, for early career postdoctoral scholars
Subject: Humanities and social sciences

438   Society for Renaissance Studies Study Fellowships

Awarding body: Society for Renaissance Studies
Address: Society for Renaissance Studies, Spanish and Latin American Studies Department, University College London, Gower St, London WC1E 6BT
Tel: 020 7679 7121
Email: a.samson@ucl.ac.uk
Web: www.rensoc.org.uk/funding/fellowships/study/apply/
Contact: Fellowships Officer
Award: Several awarded annually, value up to £1,500, to support travel expenses, for graduate students from institutions in Britain and Ireland in advanced stages of doctoral research, closing date 31 May
Objective: To support research
Subject: Renaissance studies, including history, art, architecture, philosophy, science, technology, religion, music, literature and languages

439   William Lambarde (1536–1601) Memorial Fund

Awarding body: Society of Antiquaries of London
Address: Society of Antiquaries of London, Burlington House, Piccadilly, London W1J 0BE
Tel: 020 7479 7080
Fax: 020 7287 6967
Email: Jzdunek@sal.org.uk
Web: www.sal.org.uk/grants/williamlambarde/
Contact: Research Committee
Award: Up to 4 per year, value up to £500 for travel, closing date 15 Jan
Objective: To assist travel in the field of archaeology or antiquarian studies, for non-students
Subject: Archaeology or antiquarian studies

440   Winston Churchill Memorial Trust Travel Fellowship

Awarding body: Winston Churchill Memorial Trust
Address: Winston Churchill Memorial Trust, 29 Great Smith St (Sth Door), London SW1P 3BL
Tel: 020 7799 1660
Fax: 020 7799 1667
Email: office@wcmt.org.uk
Web: www.wcmt.org.uk
Award: 125 awarded annually, value varies, but includes travel within country or countries visited, daily living and travel insurance, applications Mar to mid Oct annually
Objective: For overseas travel relating to a specific project, see categories on website
Subject: Specific areas change annually, see website

INDEX

References are to award number, not pages

1 Index of awards

AAUW International Fellowships, 20

Abba P Schwartz Research Fellowship, 97

Abraham Lincoln Brigade Archives George Watt Memorial Essay Contest, 275

A G Leventis Fellowship in Hellenic Studies, 21

Ahmad Mustafa Abu-Hakima Bursary, 188

Ahmanson-Getty Postdoctoral Fellowships, 98

Alan Pearsall Postdoctoral Fellowship in Naval and Maritime History, 160

Albin Salton Research Fellowship, 22

Albright Fellowships, 23

Alec Nove Prize, 276

Alexander Prize, 277

Alfred and Fay Chandler Book Award, 278

Alfred D Chandler Jr
– Travel Fellowship, 99
– International Visiting Scholars, 24

All Souls College Visiting Fellowships, 355

American Association for the History of Nursing Grants for Historical Research, 356

American Historical Association Prizes, Fellowships and Awards, 279

American Philosophical Society Library Resident Research Fellowships, 100

American School of Classical Studies at Athens Fellowships, 25

American Schools of Oriental Research
– Excavation Fellowships, 8
– Mesopotamian Fellowship, 9

American Society for 18th-Century Studies
– Clark Fellowships, 101
– Library Fellowships, 102
– Graduate Student Conference Paper Competition, 280
– Graduate Student Research Paper Award, 281
– Travel Grants, 426
– Travelling Jam-Pot: Fund for Graduate Students, 427

American Society of Church History Prizes, 282

Anderson Fund, 357

Andrew W Mellon Postdoctoral Fellowships in the Humanities, 26

Anglo-Danish Scholarship Awards, 27

Annibel Jenkins Biography Prize, 283

ARC Early Career Researcher Visiting Program, 28

Architectural Heritage Fund Grants and Low-Interest Loans, 10

Arthur M Schlesinger Jr Fellowship, 103

Arthur Miller Centre
– First Book Prize, 284
– Prize, 285

Arts and Humanities Research Council
– Block Grant Partnership 2, 189
– Collaborative Doctoral Awards Scheme, 190
– Fellowships Scheme, 358
– Research Grants Scheme, 359

Asia Research Institute Research Fellowships, 360

Association of Rhodes Scholars in Australia Scholarship, 29

Audrey and William H Helfand Fellowship in the History of Medicine and Public Health, 104

Aurelius Charitable Trust Grants, 144
Australian Bicentennial Scholarships and Fellowships, 30

BAAS Founders' Research Travel Award, 428
BAJS Studentship, 191
Balsdon Fellowship, 31
Barbara 'Penny' Kanner Prize, 286
Barbara Thom Postdoctoral Fellowships, 345
Beckman Center for the History of Chemistry Travel Grants, 105
Beinecke Library Visiting Fellowships, 106
Bernard Buckman Scholarship, 192
BFWG Charitable Foundation
– Emergency Grants, 193
– Main Grants, 194
Bibliographic Association of America Fellowships, 32
Birgit Baldwin Fellowship, 195
Birkbeck Research Studentships, 196
University of Birmingham College of Arts and Law Scholarships, 197
Brian Hewson Crawford Fellowship, 33
Brill Fellowship at CHASE, 361
University of Bristol Postgraduate Research Scholarships, 198
British Academy
– Ancient Persia Fund Grants, 429
– International Partnerships and Mobility, 430
– Mid-Career Fellowships, 362
– Postdoctoral Fellowships, 161
– Senior Research Fellowships, 363
– Small Research Grants, 364
British Association for American Studies
– Ambassador's Postgraduate Award, 287
– Book Prize, 288
British Association for American Studies
– Postgraduate Essay Prize, 289

– Postgraduate Short-Term Travel Awards, 431
British Association for Japanese Studies Conference Support, 1
British Association for Slavonic and East European Studies Postgraduate Research Grants, 199
British Chamber of Commerce in Germany Foundation Scholarships, 200
British Federation of Women Graduates Awards, 201
British Institute at Ankara
– Research Scholarship, 34
– Study Grants, 365
British Institute in Eastern Africa Minor Grants, 366
British School at Athens
– Early Career Fellowships, 35
– Fieldwork Bursary, 11
– Knossos Research Fund, 367
– Visiting Fellowships, 36
British School at Rome – Rome Awards, 37
Brooke Hindle Postdoctoral Fellowship, 162
Browning Fund, 368
British Society for the History of Science
– Butler-Eyles Travel Grants, 432
– Master's Degree Bursaries, 202
– Research Grants, 369
– Singer Prize, 290
– Special Projects Grants, 145
Buchan Lectures, 2

CAARI Graduate Student Fellowships, 203
Caird North American Fellowship, 107
Caird Senior Research Fellowship, 108
Caird Short-Term Research Fellowships, 109
Caledonian Scholarships, 204
Canterbury Historical and Archaeological Society Research and Publications Grant, 346

Carl Albert Congressional Research and Studies Center Visiting Scholars Program, 38
Carnegie Collaborative Larger Grants, 370
Carnegie Small Research Grants, 371
Carnegie Scholarships, 205
Catherine Macaulay Prize, 291
Center for Advanced Holocaust Studies Fellowships, 39
Center for History of Science Scholarships, 110
Challenge Funding, 12
Chalmers-Jervise Prize, 292
Chemical Heritage Foundation Fellowships, 372
CIMO Fellowships, 40
Clarendon Fund Scholarships, 206
Clark Short-Term Fellowships, 111
Clark-Huntington Joint Bibliographical Fellowship, 41
Colin Matthew Fund – Travel Awards for Historical Research, 433
Collaborative Research Grants, 373
Columbia Society of Fellows in the Humanities Postdoctoral Fellowships, 42
Commonwealth Scholarship and Fellowship Plan, 43
Council for British Research in the Levant
– Pilot Study Awards, 374
– Travel Grants, 434
– Visiting Research Fellowships and Scholarships, 44
Council for European Studies Pre-Dissertation Research Fellowships, 207
Craig Hugh Smyth Visiting Fellowship, 45
Criticos Prize, 294
Cullman Center Fellowships, 112

Daiwa Foundation
– Awards, 146
– Scholarships, 46
– Small Grants, 147

Dan David Prize Scholarships, 375
Dana and David Dornsife Fellowship, 113
David Berry Essay/History Scotland Prize, 295
David Bruce Centre
– Fellowships, 47
– Postgraduate Research and Conference Grants, 208
– Visiting European Fellowships, 48
– Visiting Junior Fellowships, 209
Deyermond Fellowship, 376
Dianne Woest Fellowship in the Arts and Humanities, 114
Dixon Ryan Fox Prize, 296
Dr A H Heineken Prize for History, 298
The Dorothy Dunnett History Prize, 297
Dover Fund, 377

Early Medieval Europe Essay Prize, 299
Eccles Centre Visiting Professorships, Fellowships and Postgraduate Awards, 115
Economic and Social Research Council Research Grants Scheme, 378
Economic History Fellowships, 163
Economic History Society
– Bursaries, 210
– Bursary Scheme for PhD Students, 211
– Facility Grants for Undergraduate Students, 148
– First Monograph Prize, 300
– Initiatives and Conference Fund, 3
– Internships at the Ashmolean Museum, Oxford, 149
– Research Fund for Graduate Students, 212
– Small Research Grants Scheme, 379
Ecumenical Patriarch Bartholomaios I Postgraduate Studentship in Byzantine Studies, 213

Elie Kedourie Memorial Fund Research Grants, 164
Elisabeth Barker Fund, 165
Émilie Du Châtelet Award for Independent Scholarship, 380
Erasmus Mundus Programme, 214
Ernest Hemingway Research Grants, 116
Essex Heritage Trust Grants, 13
European University Institute Doctoral Programme Grants, 215
Everett Helm Visiting Fellowships, 49

Fellowship Program for Advanced Social Science Research on Japan, 50
Fellowship Programs at Independent Research Institutions, 51
Finnish Studies and Research: Scholarships for Postgraduate Studies and Research at Finnish Universities, 216
Folger Shakespeare Library Research Fellowships, 52
Ford Foundation Grants and Programs, 150
Foundation for the History of Women in Medicine Fellowships, 53
Fraenkel Prize, 301
Frances A Yates
– Research Fellowships (Long-Term), 381
– Fellowships, 382
Frank Knox Fellowships at Harvard University, 54
Franklin Research Grants, 166
Frederick Burkhardt Residential Fellowships for Recently Tenured Scholars, 55
Friends of Princeton University Library Research Grants, 117
Fritz Thyssen Stiftung Support, 383

George Blazyca Prize in East European Studies, 302
George Grote Prize in Ancient History, 303

George of Cyprus and Julian Chrysostomides Bursaries, 217
Gerald Averay Wainwright Near Eastern Archaeological Fund, 384
Gerald R Ford Foundation Research Travel Grants Program, 118
Gerald R Ford Scholar Award (Dissertation Award) in Honor of Robert M Teeter, 218
German History Society Essay Prize, 304
Getty Library Research Grants, 119
Gilchrist Educational Trust Grants, 219
Gita Chaudhuri Prize, 305
Gladstone History Book Prize, 306
Gladstone's Library Scholarships, 120
The Gladys Krieble Delmas Foundation Grants for Independent Research on Venetian History and Culture, 385
Gordon Aldrick Scholarship, 220
Grants-in-Aid for Research at the Rockefeller Archive Center, 121
Grete Sondheimer Fellowship, 386
Griffith Egyptological Fund, 151
Gunning Jubilee Gift, 435

Hagley Exploratory Research Grants, 122
Hagley Prize, 307
Harry S Truman Library
– Dissertation Year Fellowship, 221
– Research Grants, 123
– Scholar's Award, 347
Harvard Postdoctoral Fellowships in Japanese Studies, 56
Harvard-Newcomen Postdoctoral Fellowship, 167
Hayek Fund for Scholars, 387
Hellenic Society Council Grants, 152
Hemlow Prize in Burney Studies, 308
Henri Frankfort Research Fellowship, 388
Henrietta Larson Article Award, 309
Henry Belin du Pont
– Dissertation Fellowship, 222

– Fellowships, 124
Henry Moore Institute Research
  Fellowships, 57
Heritage Grants, 14
Historic Society of Lancashire and
  Cheshire
– Publication Grants, 348
– Research Grants, 389
Hosei International Fund Foreign
  Scholars Fellowship, 58
Hoskins Duffield Fund, 223
Houghton Library Visiting Fellowships,
  125
Hugh Last and Donald Atkinson
  Funds, 349
Hugh Last Fellowship, 59
Hugh Le May Fellowship, 60
Humane Studies Fellowships, 389
Humboldt Research Fellowship
– for Experienced Researchers, 61
– for Postdoctoral Researchers, 168
Huntington Research Awards, 62

Institute for Advanced Studies in the
  Humanities (IASH)
– Postdoctoral Bursaries, 169
– Visiting Research Fellowships, 170
– SSPS Visiting Research
  Fellowships, 171
IEEE Life Members' Fellowship in
  Electrical History, 390
Institute for Humane Studies Summer
  Graduate Research Fellowships,
  224
Institute for Medieval Studies MA and
  PhD Bursaries, 225
Institute of Classical Studies Visiting
  Fellowships, 391
Institute of Historical Research
– Junior Research Fellowships, 226
– Postgraduate Bursaries, 227
International Medieval Bibliography
  Bursary, 228
Italian Government Awards, 63
Ivan Morris Memorial Prize, 310

J B Harley Research Fellowships in
  the History of Cartography, 126
J Franklin Jameson Fellowship in
  American History, 127
Jacob Rader Marcus Center
  Fellowship Program, 64
Jacobite Studies Trust Fellowships in
  History, 392
James L Clifford Prize, 293
Janet Arnold Award, 393
Japanese Association of University
  Women (JAUW) International
  Fellowship, 65
Japanese Government (MEXT)
  Scholarships for Research
  Students, 66
Jean Monnet Programme, 153
Jesus College
– Graduate Scholarships, 229
– Research/Book Allowances, 230
The Joan Mervyn Hussey Prize in
  Byzantine Studies, 311
John Ben Snow Prize, 312
John Crump Studentship, 231
John D Lees Memorial Bursary, 232
John J Pisano Travel Grants, 436
John Leyerle-CARA Prize for
  Dissertation Research, 313
John Morrison Memorial Fund for
  Hellenic Maritime Studies, 394
John Nicholas Brown Prize, 314
The John Penrose Barron Prize in
  Hellenic Studies, 315
Judith Lee Ridge Article Prize, 316
Julian Corbett Prize in Modern Naval
  History, 317

Kanner Fellowship in British Studies,
  128
Katherine F Pantzer Jr Fellowship in
  Descriptive Bibliography, 129
Kennedy Memorial Trust
  Scholarships, 67
Kennedy Research Grants, 130
Kenneth Lindsay Scholarship Trust
  Grants, 68
Kerr History Prize, 318

Larry J Hackman Research Residency Program, 396
Lavinia L Dock Award, 319
University of Leeds
— Department of Philosophy Scholarships, 237
— Fee Scholarships, 233
— Research Scholarships, 234
— School of History Master's Scholarships, 235
— School of History PhD Scholarship, 236
Leiden University Excellence Scholarship Programme, 238
Lemmermann Foundation Scholarships, 69
Leverhulme Trust
— Early Career Fellowships, 172
— Emeritus Fellowships, 398
— International Academic Fellowships, 399
— International Networks, 400
— Major Research Fellowships, 401
— Research Fellowships, 397
— Research Project Grants, 402
— Study Abroad Studentships, 70
Lifelong Learning Programme: Erasmus, 154
London School of Economics Funding, 239
Louis Gottschalk Prize, 320

Macmillan-Rodewald Studentship, 403
Marc Raeff Book Prize, 321
Margaret and Tom Jones Fund, 15
Marjorie Kovler Fellowship, 131
Mark Samuels Lasner Fellowship in Printing History, 404
Mary Adelaide Nutting Award, 322
Mary M Roberts Award, 323
Medieval Academy Dissertation Grants, 240
Mellon Fellowships in the Humanities, 71
Mellon Postdoctoral Fellowship, 132

Mellon Visiting Fellowship, 72
Mellon-CES Dissertation Completion Fellowship, 241
Melvin Kranzberg Dissertation Fellowship, 242
Mendel Fellowships, 73
Metropolitan Museum of Art
— Fellowships, 74
— Internships, 155
Meyricke Graduate Scholarships, 243
Michael Nicholson Thesis Prize, 324
Michael Ventris Memorial Award, 405
Michigan Society of Fellows Postdoctoral Fellowships in the Humanities, Arts, Sciences and Professions, 173
Middlesex University Postgraduate Scholarships, 244
Midland History Prize, 325
Mitchell Prize for Research on Early British Serials, 326
Murray Prize for History, 327

NASA Fellowship in Aerospace History, 406
National Endowment for the Humanities Fellowships/Faculty Research Awards, 407
National Humanities Center Fellowships, 75
Neil Ker Memorial Fund, 174
New Zealand History Research Trust Fund Awards, 408
New Zealand Oral History Awards, 409
Newberry Library Short-Term Fellowships, 133
Newby Trust Postdoctoral Bursary, 175
Newton International Fellowships, 76
Nikolaos Oikonomides Postgraduate Studentship in Byzantine Studies, 245
Northcote Graduate Scholarships, 246
Norwegian Research Council Yggdrasil Mobility Programme, 77

Nuffield College Postdoctoral Prize Research Fellowships, 410
NWO Rubicon Scholarship, 78

Omohundro Institute Postdoctoral Fellowship, 350
Organization of American Historians Awards, 328
Oscar Kenshur Book Prize, 329
Our Heritage, 16

Pantzer Senior Fellowship, 79
Pasold Research Fund, 156
Past and Present Postdoctoral Fellowship in History, 176
Pat Macklin Memorial Bursaries in Hellenic and Byzantine Studies, 247
Paul Klemperer Fellowship in the History of Medicine, 134
Paul Mellon Centre Rome Fellowship, 80
Pembroke Center Postdoctoral Fellowships, 177
Phillips Fund Grants for Native American Research, 411
University of Plymouth – Graduate School Scholarships (PhD), 248
The Pollard Prize (sponsored by Wiley-Blackwell), 330
Pontifical Institute of Mediaeval Studies Postdoctoral Mellon Fellowships, 178

Radcliffe Institute Fellowships, 81
Random House Scholarship, 249
University of Reading Postgraduate Research Studentships, 250
Research Grants for Getty Scholars and Visiting Scholars; Pre- and Postdoctoral Fellowships, 82
Residencies at the Rockefeller Foundation Bellagio Center, 83
Rhodes Postdoctoral Fellowship, 179
Rhodes University Andrew Mellon Postdoctoral Fellowship, 180
Richard Bradford McConnell Fund for Landscape Studies, 412

Richard Chattaway Scholarship, 251
Richard III Society and Yorkist History Trust Bursary, 252
Robert and Lisa Sainsbury Fellowships, 413
Robert H Smith International Center for Jefferson Studies Short-Term Fellowships, 84
Robert Kiln Charitable Trust Grants, 17
Robert M Kingdon Fellowship in Judeo-Christian Religious Studies, 85
Robert Sainsbury Scholarship, 253
Robert Schuman Scholarships, 86
Rome Scholarships and Fellowships in Ancient, Medieval and Later Italian Studies, 87
Rooke Memorial Prize, 331
Roosevelt Institute Grants-in-Aid, 135
Royal Historical Society
– Conference Assistance, 4
– Postgraduate Research Grants, 254
– Training and Conference Bursaries, 255
Royal Historical Society/*History Today* Prize, 332
The Royal Society of Literature Jerwood Awards, 351
Royal Society Research Grants, 414
Rydon Fellowship in Australian Politics and Political History, 181

Sackler Short-Term Research Fellowships, 136
Sackler-Caird Fellowship, 137
Sainsbury Research Unit for the Arts of Africa, Oceania and the Americas
– MA Scholarships, 256
– Visiting Fellowships, 88
University of St Andrews School of History MLitt Awards, 257
St Hilda's College Graduate Scholarships, 258
St John's College Benefactors' Scholarships for Research, 259

Schallek Fellowship and Awards, 260
Schlesinger Library
– History of Women in America
Dissertation Grants, 138
– History of Women Research
Support Grants, 139
Scholarly Edition Grants, 352
Schomburg Center Scholars in
Residence, 89
School of Historical Studies
Membership, 90
School of Oriental and African Studies
– Doctoral Scholarships, 261
– Doctoral Scholarships – Faculty of
Arts and Humanities, 262
Scouloudi Historical Awards, 353
Sean W Dever Memorial Prize, 333
Sharing Heritage, 18
Shelby Cullom Davis Center for
Historical Studies Research
Fellowships, 91
Sheldon Memorial Trust
– Essay Prize, 334
– Publications Grants, 354
SHOT-NASA Fellowship in the History
of Space Technology, 182
Sino-British Fellowship Trust, 415
Sir Ernest Cassel Educational Trust
Fund Grants, 437
Sir Francis Hill Scholarships, 263
Sir John Neale Prize in Tudor History,
335
Sir John Plumb Charitable Trust, 416
Sir Richard Stapley Educational Trust
Grants, 264
Society for Renaissance Studies
– Postdoctoral Fellowships, 183
– Study Fellowships, 438
Society for the Humanities
Fellowships, 92
Society for the Study of French
History
– Conference Bursaries, 5
– Conference Grants, 6
– Research Grants, 265
Society of Antiquaries of London

Research Grants, 417
Society of Antiquaries of Scotland
– Bursaries for Young Fellows
Attending Conferences, 7
– Research Grants, 418
Solmsen Postdoctoral Fellowships, 93
Stanford Humanities Center External
Faculty Fellowships, 94
Stanley Burton Research
Scholarships, 266
Stansky Book Prize, 336
Stein-Arnold Exploration Fund
Research Grants, 184
Stetten Memorial Fellowship in the
History of Biomedical Sciences and
Technology, 185
Stirling Funding, 267
Susan Strange Book Prize, 337

T E Lawrence Award, 268
Tebbutt Research Fund, 419
Teresa E Christy Award, 338
Tessa and Mortimer Wheeler
Memorial Fund, 19
Theodora Bosanquet Bursaries, 140
Theodore C Sorensen Fellowship,
420
Thirsk-Feinstein PhD Dissertation
Prize, 339
Thomas K McCraw Fellowship in US
Business History, 95
Tilburg University Scholarship
Program, 269
Tomlin Fund, 157
Toshiba International Foundation
Graduate Research Studentship,
270
T S Ashton Prize, 340

University College London
– Fees Scholarships for MA
Programmes, 271
– History Department Research/
Teaching Studentship, 272

Van Courtlandt Elliott Prize, 341
Villa I Tatti Fellowships, 186
Vronwy Hankey Memorial Fund, 421

Walter D Love Prize, 342
Wardrop Fund for Georgian
  (Transcaucasia) Studies, 422
Wellcome Trust Awards, Fellowships
  and Studentships, 158
Western Association of Women
  Historians Founders Dissertation
  Fellowship, 273
The White House Historical
  Association Research Grants, 423
Whitfield Prize, 343
William Lambarde (1536–1601)
  Memorial Fund, 439
William R Miller Graduate Awards,
  274
Winston Churchill Memorial Trust
  Travel Fellowship, 440
Winterthur Dissertation Fellowships,
  141
Winterthur Research Fellowships, 142
University of Wisconsin-Madison
  Grants-in-Aid, 143
Wolfson College
– Non-Stipendiary Junior Research
  Fellowships, 187
– Non-Stipendiary Research
  Fellowships, 424
– Stipendiary Junior Research
  Fellowship, 425
Wolfson Foundation Grants, 159
Wolfson History Prize, 344
Wyndham Deedes Memorial Travel
  Scholarship, 96

2   Index of awarding bodies

Abraham Lincoln Brigade Archives (ALBA) (USA), 275

Alexander von Humboldt Foundation (Germany), 61, 168

All Souls College – University of Oxford, 355

American Association for the History of Nursing (AAHN) (USA), 319, 322, 323, 338, 356

American Association of University Women (AAUW) (USA), 20

American Council of Learned Societies (ACLS) (USA), 55

American Historical Association (AHA) (USA), 127, 279, 406

American Philosophical Society (USA), 100, 166, 411

American Printing History Association (APHA) (USA), 404

American School of Classical Studies at Athens (ASCSA) (Greece), 25

American Schools of Oriental Research (ASOR) (USA), 8, 9

American Society for 18th-Century Studies (ASECS) (USA), 102, 280, 281, 291, 293, 308, 320, 380, 426, 427, 283

American Society of Church History (USA), 282

Anglo-Danish Society, 27

Anglo-Israel Association, 68, 96

ARC Centre of Excellence in the History of Emotions (Europe 1100–1800) (Australia), 28

Architectural Heritage Fund, 10

Arthur Miller Centre for American Studies – University of East Anglia, 284, 285

Arts and Humanities Research Council (AHRC), 189, 190, 358, 359

Asia Research Institute – National University of Singapore (Singapore), 360

Association of Commonwealth Universities (ACU), 43

Association of Rhodes Scholars in Australia (Australia), 29

Aurelius Charitable Trust, 144

Beinecke Rare Book and Manuscript Library (USA), 106

BFWG Charitable Foundation, 140, 193, 194

Bibliographic Association of America (USA), 32, 79, 326

Birkbeck – University of London, 196

University of Birmingham, 197

University of Bristol, 198

British Academy, 161, 164, 165, 174, 184, 362–4, 368, 415, 429, 430, 437

British Association for American Studies (BAAS), 115, 287–9, 428, 431

British Association for Japanese Studies (BAJS), 1, 191, 231, 270, 310, 413

British Association for Slavonic and East European Studies (BASEES), 199, 276, 302

British Chamber of Commerce in Germany Foundation (Germany), 200

British Federation of Women Graduates (BFWG), 201

British Institute at Ankara (BIAA), 34, 365

British Institute in Eastern Africa (Kenya), 366

British International Studies Association, 324, 337

British School at Athens (BSA) (Greece), 11, 21, 35, 36, 367, 395, 403, 412, 421

British School at Rome (BSR), 31, 37, 59, 87

British Society for the History of Science (BSHS), 145, 202, 290, 331, 369, 432

Brown University (USA), 177

Canterbury Historical and Archaeological Society, 346

Carl Albert Congressional Research and Studies Center (USA), 38

Carnegie Trust for the Universities of Scotland, 204, 205, 370, 371

Center for Advanced Holocaust Studies – United States Holocaust Memorial Museum (USHMM) (USA), 39

Center for Eighteenth-Century Studies at Indiana University (ASECS) (USA), 329

Center for History of Science (Centrum för Vetenskapshistoria) – Royal Swedish Academy of Sciences (Sweden), 110

Centre for International Mobility (CIMO) (Finland), 40, 216

Chemical Heritage Foundation (CHF) (USA), 105, 372

Clarendon Fund, 206

Colin Matthew Fund Committee, 433

Columbia University Society of Fellows in the Humanities (USA), 42

Council for British Archaeology (CBA), 12

Council for British Research in the Levant (CBRL), 44, 374, 434

Council for European Studies (CES) (USA), 207, 241

Cyprus American Archaeological Research Institute (CAARI) (USA), 203

Daiwa Anglo-Japanese Foundation, 46, 146, 147

Dan David Prize/Tel Aviv University (Israel), 375

David Bruce Centre for American Studies – Keele University, 47, 48, 208, 209, 232

Department of Philosophy – University of Leeds, 237

Dorothy and Lewis B Cullman Center for Scholars and Writers – New York Public Library (USA), 112

The Dorothy Dunnett Society, Centre for Medieval and Renaissance Studies, University of Edinburgh, 297

University of East Anglia, 88, 253, 256

Economic and Social Research Council (ESRC), 378

Economic History Society, 3, 148, 149, 210–12, 300, 339, 340, 379

Edwin O Reischauer Institute of Japanese Studies – Harvard University (USA), 56

Eighteenth-Century Russian Studies Association (ECRSA) (USA), 321

Essex Heritage Trust, 13

European Commission (Belgium), 153

European Parliament, 86

European Union, 154, 214

European University Institute, 215

Folger Shakespeare Library (USA), 52

Ford Foundation (USA), 150

Foundation for the History of Women in Medicine (USA), 53

Friends of the UW-Madison Libraries (USA), 143

Fritz Thyssen Stiftung für Wissenschaftsförderung (Germany), 383

Gerald R Ford Foundation (USA), 118, 218

German History Society, 304

Getty Foundation (USA), 82, 119

Gilchrist Educational Trust, 219

Gladstone's Library, 120

Gladys Krieble Delmas Foundation (USA), 385

Hagley Museum and Library (USA), 122, 124, 222, 307

Harry S Truman Library Institute (USA), 123, 221, 123, 347

Harvard Business School (USA), 24, 95, 99, 167, 278, 309

Hellenic Institute – Royal Holloway, University of London, 213, 217, 245, 247, 311, 315

Hellenic Society, 152, 377

Henry Moore Institute, 57

Heritage Lottery Fund, 14, 16, 18

Historic New Orleans Collection (USA), 114

Historic Society of Lancashire and Cheshire, 348, 389

Hosei University (Japan), 58

Houghton Library – Harvard University (USA), 125, 129

Huntington Library, Art Collections and Botanical Gardens (USA), 62, 113, 132, 345

IEEE (USA), 391

Institute for Advanced Studies in the Humanities (IASH), 169, 170, 175

Institute for Advanced Studies in the Humanities (IASH) and School of Social and Political Science (SSPS), University of Edinburgh, 171

Institute for Advanced Study, School of Historical Studies (USA), 90

Institute for Humane Studies (IHS) – George Mason University (USA), 224, 387, 390

Institute for Medieval Studies – University of Leeds, 225, 228

Institute for Research in the Humanities (USA), 85, 93

Institute of Classical Studies – University of London, 303, 391, 405

Institute of Historical Research (IHR) – University of London, 71, 160, 163, 176, 226, 227, 252, 317, 330, 335, 353, 393

Italian Cultural Institute, 63

J B Harley Fellowships, 126

Jacob Rader Marcus Center of the American Jewish Archives (USA), 64

Japanese Association of University Women (JAUW) (Japan), 65

Japanese Ministry of Education, Culture, Sports, Science and Technology (MEXT), 66

Japan-US Friendship Commission/ National Endowment for the Humanities (NEH) (USA), 50

Jesus College – University of Oxford, 229, 230, 243, 268

John F Kennedy Library Foundation (USA), 97, 103, 116, 130, 131, 420

Kennedy Memorial Trust, 67

University of Leeds, 233, 234, 266

University of Leicester, Centre for English Local History, 223

Leiden University (The Netherlands), 238

Lemmermann Foundation (Italy), 69

Leverhulme Trust, 70, 172, 397–402

Lilly Library, Indiana University (USA), 49, 73

London Hellenic Society, 294

London School of Economics (LSE) – University of London, 239

Medieval Academy of America (USA), 195, 240, 260, 313, 314, 341

Menzies Centre for Australian Studies – King's College London, 30, 181

Metropolitan Museum of Art (USA), 74, 155

Michigan Society of Fellows (USA), 173

Middlesex University, 244

Midland History – University of Birmingham, 325

National Endowment for the
Humanities (NEH) (USA), 51, 352,
373, 407
National Humanities Center (USA), 75
National Institutes of Health (USA),
185, 436
National Maritime Museum/John
Carter Brown Library (USA), 107
National Maritime Museum/Royal
Observatory Greenwich, 108, 109,
136, 137
Netherlands Organisation for
Scientific Research (NWO) (The
Netherlands), 78
New York Academy of Medicine
(USA), 104, 134
New York State Archives (USA), 396
New York State Historical Association
(USA), 296, 318
New Zealand – Ministry for Culture
and Heritage, 408, 409
Newberry Library (USA), 133
Newton International Fellowships
(Royal Society and British
Academy), 76
North American Conference on British
Studies (NACBS) (USA), 312, 336,
342
Northcote Graduate Scholarships, 246
Norwegian Research Council, 77
University of Nottingham, 263
Nuffield College – University of
Oxford, 410

Omohundro Institute of Early
American History and Culture
(OIEAHC) (USA), 350
Organization of American Historians
(OAH) (USA), 328
Oriental Institute – University of
Oxford, 151, 384, 422

Pasold Research Fund, 156
The Paul Mellon Centre for Studies in
British Art, 80
Pembroke College – University of
Oxford, 220

Penn Humanities Forum – University
of Pennsylvania (USA), 26
University of Plymouth, 248
Pontifical Institute of Mediaeval
Studies (Canada), 178
President and Fellows of Harvard
College, 54
Princeton University Library (USA),
117

Radcliffe Institute for Advanced Study
– Harvard University (USA), 81
University of Reading, 250
Rhodes University (South Africa), 60,
179, 180
Robert H Smith International Center
for Jefferson Studies (USA), 84
Robert Kiln Charitable Trust, 17
Rockefeller Archive Center (USA),
121
Rockefeller Foundation (USA), 83
Roman Society, 349
Roosevelt Institute (USA), 135
Royal Historical Society, 4, 254, 255,
277, 295, 306, 332, 343
The Royal Netherlands Academy
of Arts and Sciences (The
Netherlands), 298
Royal Society, 414
Royal Society of Literature, 351

University of St Andrews, 257
St Catherine's College – University of
Oxford, 249
St Edmund Hall – University of
Oxford, 274
St Hilda's College – University of
Oxford, 258
St John's College – University of
Cambridge, 259
Schlesinger Library (USA), 138, 139
Schomburg Center for Research in
Black Culture (USA), 89
School of History – University of
Leeds, 235, 236

School of Oriental and African Studies
(SOAS) – University of London, 188,
192, 261, 262
Shelby Cullom Davis Center for
Historical Studies (USA), 91
Sheldon Memorial Trust, 334, 354
Sir John Plumb Charitable Trust, 416
Sir Richard Stapley Educational Trust,
264
Society for Nautical Research, 157,
357
Society for Renaissance Studies, 183,
438
Society for the History of Technology
(SHOT) (USA), 162, 182, 242
Society for the Humanities (USA), 92
Society for the Study of French
History, 5, 6, 265
Society of Antiquaries of London, 2,
7, 15, 19, 292, 327, 394, 417, 418,
435, 439
Stanford Humanities Center (USA), 94
University of Stirling, 267

Tilburg University (The Netherlands),
269

UCLA Center for 17th- and 18th-
Century Studies (USA), 41, 98, 101,
111, 128, 251, 271, 272

Villa I Tatti (Italy), 45, 72, 186

W F Albright Institute of
Archaeological Research (USA),
23, 333
Warburg Institute – University of
London, 22, 33, 361, 376, 381, 382,
386, 388
Wealden Iron Research Group
(WIRG), 419
Wellcome Trust, 158
Western Association of Women
Historians (WAWH) (USA), 286,
273, 305, 316
White House Historical Association
(USA), 423

The Wiener Library for the Study of
the Holocaust and Genocide, 301
Wiley-Blackwell Publishing Ltd, 299
Winston Churchill Memorial Trust, 440
Winterthur Museum, Garden and
Library (USA), 141, 142
Wolfson College – University of
Oxford, 187, 424, 425
Wolfson Foundation, 159, 344

3   Geographical index

Africa, 88, 151, 256, 366

Asia, 1, 46, 56, 146, 147, 184, 191,
192, 220, 231, 270, 310, 413, 415

Britain, 2, 7, 13, 14, 41, 128, 149, 223,
252, 260, 292, 295, 312, 327, 336,
342, 343, 348, 368, 389, 418, 419,
435

Europe, 5, 6, 9, 11, 21, 31, 34, 35–7,
45, 59, 63, 69, 72, 80, 85–7, 93,
152, 153, 165, 174, 186, 195, 199,
203, 207, 215, 216, 241, 265, 275,
276, 301–4, 321, 331, 349, 353,
365, 367, 376, 377, 385, 395, 403,
405, 412, 421, 422

Latin America, 103

Middle East, 8, 23, 44, 68, 96, 164,
188, 213, 217, 245, 247, 311, 315,
333, 361, 374, 388, 429, 434

North America, 47, 48, 64, 84, 114,
115, 118, 121–4, 127, 130–2, 138,
139, 141, 142, 208–9, 218, 221,
222, 232, 284, 285, 287–9, 296,
307, 318, 328, 344, 347, 350, 396,
411, 420, 423, 428, 431

Pacific, 30, 181, 408, 409

World, 22, 267

4 Subject index

Ancient history, 9, 33, 59, 184, 213, 217, 245, 247, 311, 315, 349, 388, 392, 417, 421, 439

Archaeology, 2, 7, 11, 12, 15, 17, 19, 21, 23, 25, 31, 36, 37, 87, 151, 196, 203, 292, 303, 333, 346, 348, 367, 384, 389, 403, 405, 417–19, 435, 439

Art and architecture, 10, 55, 57, 63, 74, 80, 82, 88, 119, 141, 142, 155, 156, 253, 256, 266

Business history, 24, 95, 122, 167, 278, 307, 309

Byzantine history, 213, 217, 245, 247, 294, 311, 315

Cartography, 126

Conservation, 74, 155, 394

Cultural history, 22, 46, 69, 80, 88, 115, 128, 141, 142, 146, 147, 152, 216, 220, 253, 256, 266, 275, 280, 281, 284, 287–9, 291, 293, 308, 321, 376, 377, 380–2, 386, 394, 413, 420, 426–8, 431

Economic history, 3, 24, 95, 99, 148, 149, 163, 210–12, 278, 300, 309, 339, 340, 379

Environmental history, 395

Ethnic/Migration history, 89, 97, 216, 350, 411

Gender and women's history, 53, 138, 139, 286, 291, 305, 380

History, general, 4–7, 11, 25, 26, 28, 31–3, 36–9, 41, 47, 48, 52, 55, 62, 69, 79, 86, 87, 90, 91, 98, 100–3, 106, 111, 113–16, 121, 124, 127, 128, 130, 132, 135, 140, 151, 156, 157, 165, 176, 178, 183, 184, 188, 196, 197, 199, 208, 209, 215, 222, 225, 226–8, 232, 235–7, 252, 254, 255, 263, 265, 267, 268, 271–3, 276, 277, 279, 280, 281, 283–5, 287–9, 292, 294–9, 301–4, 306, 312, 316, 318, 320, 326–8, 330, 332, 335, 336, 342–5, 348–50, 353, 357, 361, 368, 375, 384, 388, 389, 392, 393, 396, 403, 405, 406, 408, 411, 416, 418, 421, 422, 426–8, 431, 433, 435, 438, 440

Holocaust, 64, 249

Humanities, 8, 21, 34, 42, 44, 45, 49–51, 54, 58, 60, 71–3, 75, 82, 85, 92–4, 114, 125, 129, 133, 143, 144, 159, 161, 169, 170, 173, 175, 179, 180, 186, 187, 189, 190, 224, 258, 261, 285, 331, 352, 358–60, 362–6, 373, 374, 383, 385, 387, 390, 401, 407, 412, 415, 424, 425, 430, 434, 437

Imperial and colonial history, 98

Intellectual history, 22, 376, 381, 382, 386

International history, 46, 146, 147, 324, 337

Local history, 13, 17, 223, 325, 346

Medical history, 53, 62, 104, 113, 132, 134, 158, 319, 322, 323, 338, 345, 356

Military history, 157, 160, 251, 275, 317, 357

Oral history, 14, 409

Philosophy of history, 237

Political history, 38, 103, 118, 123, 131, 164, 171, 218, 221, 232, 267, 347, 396, 420

Religious history, 23, 120, 249, 282, 333

Science and technology, 105, 110, 145, 162, 182, 185, 202, 242, 290, 369, 372, 391, 406, 414, 432, 436

Social sciences, 3, 34, 39, 44, 58, 97, 112, 122, 138, 139, 148, 150, 161, 163, 171, 176, 187, 189, 190, 210–12, 224, 258, 300, 339, 340, 358, 359, 361–5, 374, 378, 379, 387, 390, 410, 412, 415, 424, 425, 430, 434, 437

Unrestricted, 1, 20, 27, 29, 30, 35, 40, 43, 61, 65–8, 70, 76–8, 81, 83, 96, 117, 153, 154, 166, 168, 172, 177, 181, 191, 193, 194, 198, 200, 201, 204–7, 214, 219, 229, 230, 231, 234, 238, 239, 241, 243, 244, 246, 248, 250, 257, 259, 262, 264, 269, 270, 274, 310, 351, 355, 370, 371, 397–9, 400, 402